THE DESOLATE ANTARCTIC

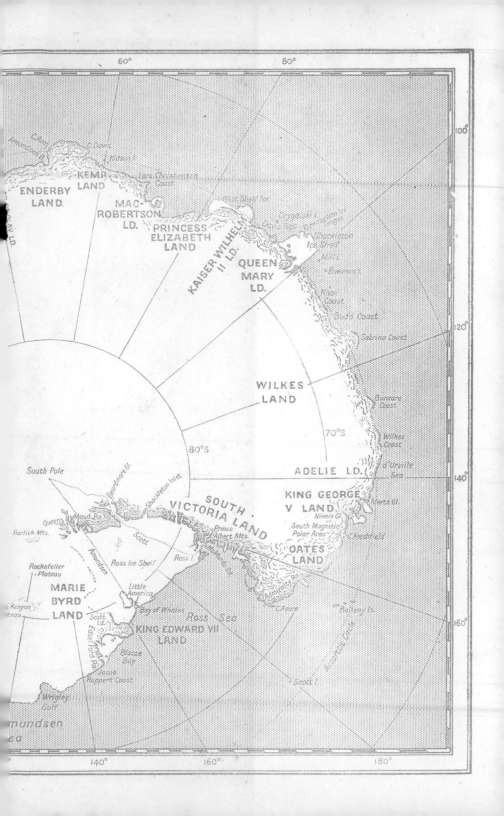

THE
DESOLATE ANTARCTIC

by

ADMIRAL LORD MOUNTEVANS

THE TRAVEL BOOK CLUB
121 CHARING CROSS ROAD
LONDON W.C.2

Printed in Great Britain by The Whitefriars Press Ltd.,
London and Tonbridge

Dedicated in great affection

to

THE RT. HON. C. R. ATTLEE, C.H., P.C.

ACKNOWLEDGMENT

Acknowledgment is made to the following Publishers for permission to quote certain passages from:

The Voyage of the Discovery by Capt. R. F. Scott. JOHN MURRAY

Scott's Last Expedition by Capt. R. F. Scott. JOHN MURRAY

The Polar Regions by R. N. Rudmose Brown. METHUEN

The Conquest of the South Pole by J. Gordon Hayes. EYRE & SPOTTISWOODE

Southern Lights by John Rymill. CHATTO & WINDUS

Beyond Horizons by Lincoln Ellsworth. WILLIAM HEINEMANN

Voyages of a Modern Viking by Helmer Hanssen. ROUTLEDGE

The Book of Polar Exploration by Edith L. Elias. GEORGE G. HARRAP

South with Scott by Lord Mountevans. COLLINS

More than forty years ago, when a very young officer in the Royal Navy, I had the great good fortune to be selected to serve in the National Antarctic Relief Expedition.

It was rather an unusual experience for a junior sub-lieutenant to be called upon suddenly to take charge as second officer in a small but heavily sparred " windjammer ". This, however, was my lot, and I was confronted by many problems which were quite strange to me, such as " wearing ship " during the still watches of the night, with only four seamen besides the man at the wheel.

We had a wonderful skipper in our little ship, the old Norwegian auxiliary barque *Morning*, for William Colbeck was a seaman by instinct as well as a man of high education and vigorous mentality.

This was in the years 1902–4, when the little *Morning* searched out and found the *Discovery* in her ice-girt winter quarters, rendered assistance in the matter of reprovisioning her, and conveyed her sick from the frozen regions of the south to the milder, kinder climate of beautiful New Zealand.

In 1910 I was appointed as second-in-command of Scott's last Antarctic expedition and given command of the old Dundee whaler, *Terra Nova*, which ship I fitted out for service in that never-to-be-forgotten enterprise.

At the end of January 1949 I was invited to write a book on the Antarctic, a subject very dear to my heart, but, as I pointed out to the publishers, I had so many commitments that unless I went into hiding I could not find time and, what is more, I should not do justice to the bearded, beaver-hatted whaling folk and others who had helped so much to open up the Great White Way to the desolate Antarctic for the explorer. It was the Southern Sealing Fleet and then, to a far greater degree, the Antarctic Whaling Fleet that furnished us with the vital information that led to scientific exploration and research within the Antarctic Circle.

Fortunately, I speak and read Norwegian, and still more fortunately I was able to purchase all three volumes of *Fangst og Forskning i Sydishavet* (" Capture and Exploration in the Icy Southern Seas ") by Bjarne Aagaard, whom I had hoped to meet, partly with a view to translating his book to the advantage of our two nations and to " Antarctics " generally. However, greatly to my regret, Bjarne Aagaard died just before I came to Norway, but I now read in his foreword that that famous Norwegian shipowner, Consul Lars Christensen, whose generous help has made the publication of this Antarctic classic possible, has himself arranged for the translation and publication in English to be carried out in America. I only hope that it will be as speedily accomplished as the writing of *The Desolate Antarctic*. I doubt it !

Anyway, I left England on Saturday, February 5, arrived in Oslo on Monday, February 7, went by train to Harpefoss in Gudbrandsdalen on Sunday, February 13, motoring to Golaa that evening, and, whilst my wife was getting her family's hut in order, I unpacked a trunk full of Antarctic books and set them out on a long wooden peasant table, in an orderly fashion as a surgeon and an intelligent nurse would lay out instruments—Cheatle forceps, dressings and so forth—all ready for a major operation. Then I helped get Andvords Hut in order, had supper and went out on to the veranda to enjoy the view of the Northern Fairyland.

It was full moon and the view of the pretty Norwegian

mountains and silver-white carpeted forests gleaming to the north and west and then faint Aurora playing in the sky made me think, as I have so often thought in this atmosphere of peace and quiet :

> The happiest heart that ever beat
> Was in some quiet breast
> That found the common daylight sweet
> And left to heaven the rest.

I could quite easily substitute " moonlight " for " daylight ", but what matter ?

Anyway, the next two days I spent on ski, which helped—it gave me, in the long climbs up the sides of the snowclad hills, time to think out this book. It was not to be a history of the Antarctic containing half a million words as such a work must do, but a book for people of all ages from ten to a hundred; a book written from experience by a sailor-explorer who believes in adventure, youth and duty, a belief in all three of which is necessary if one wishes to make an extended visit to this cruel, silent continent.

Two days later I sat on a hard wooden seat and faced the big row of Antarctic books, and then I am not sure whether I appreciated the situation or situated the appreciation—I think the latter—for I had only thirty-four days in which to write the book. I planned to work from eleven till one, and from 8 p.m. until 11 p.m., which would give me as much time for ski-ing as I wanted; but very often I worked far into the night, and on Sunday evening, March 13, or rather early on Monday morning, I woke up my wife and told her I had finished the job !

I had really been undisturbed, for we have no telephone in the mountains.

We returned to Oslo on March 16, and after ten days' enjoyment returned to England to contend with voluminous correspondence and commitments. And then my industrious secretary, Mrs. Farrell, told me in no uncertain terms that if I wished to hand in the typescript of this book to time, I must literally shut myself up and dictate from my unreadable notes for at least ten hours a day. If I agreed I could be certain of handing in typescript, illustrations and maps according to plan.

For those who are interested, I have placed a list of the books consulted in the Appendix. Some were purchased, some were gifts, and others were borrowed from the Royal Geographical Society.

K. C. Jordan drew the excellent maps to illustrate the narrative and Paul Popper supplied most of the photographs.

Andvords Hut,
   Golaa, Gudbrandsdalen,
      In the Norwegian mountains.
   1949.

CONTENTS

LIST OF ILLUSTRATIONS

Chapter One

COLD

THOSE of us who have been privileged to see the film *Scott of the Antarctic* realize the vastness of the Antarctic Continent, approaching as it does nearly four million square miles in area, counting the ice-capped inland plateaux, the coastal areas and the permanent Ice Barriers alone. In the winter months a mere conjecture would add another million square miles of hard-frozen sea surface strong enough to bear laden motor lorries and aircraft.

Looking at the general chart of the Antarctic regions, one sees that in half a dozen places the continent protrudes beyond the Antarctic Circle, 66° 33' S. latitude, and I think the little-navigated waters lying between 60° S. and the Antarctic Circle itself might well be included in the Antarctic region, for they abound with icebergs, ice shelves, floes and enormous fields of pack ice in summer and in winter. Further inspection of the chart shows several island groups like the South Sandwich Islands, South Georgia, South Orkneys, South Shetlands, Elephant Island, Coronation Island, Laurie Island, Drygalski Island and quite an archipelago about Graham Land. All the islands mentioned, except those in the Bellingshausen Sea, or west side of Graham Land, lie north of the Antarctic Circle, but they have mostly the same characteristics as Scott Island, the Balleny Group and the islands charted by the British naval explorer Sir James Clark Ross more than 100 years ago.

These far southern islands are so bleak and inhospitable that Bouvet Island, which is only in latitude

55° S., has a heavy ice cap and might well be a couple of degrees within the Antarctic Circle instead of more than 11° N. of it. I visited Bouvet as a Vice-Admiral in H.M.S. *Milford*, and felt the icy bite of the desolate Antarctic winds, which reminded me of a statement made by the late Professor Sir Edgeworth David who said that " If the whole of the Antarctic ice-cap were to be melted and run into the southern ocean it would send up the surface of the sea throughout the world as much as thirty feet and put all our piers and jetties under water."

Yes, the Antarctic Continent is indeed a desolate land ; there are no woods and pastures, no prairies or navigable rivers, no ruins of secret cities, nor monasteries perched on the tops of the mountains, no Great Walls made by man, no Pyramids or traces of ancient civilization, nothing to remind us of humanity. Why ? Because the desolate Antarctic is still, as it were, in the Ice Age.

Coal, fossils of pine trees and other wood, fossils of plants, shells and small marine animals indicate that a more moderate climate has prevailed in the unrecorded past, but Antarctica has never been inhabited. And, except for a few seals that have made their way some little distance inland—probably to die—and the Emperor penguins that seem content in small numbers to spend the winter at the edge of the Great Ice Barrier as far as 78° S., no mammals or birds are to be found on this ice-bound continent, except in the summer months.

The Antarctic is not self-supporting, nor is it likely to become so. In fact, the great deserts like the Sahara, the Gobi and the Kalahari are fertile in comparison with this hard-frozen land.

And now let us sort out the highlands and the lowlands, the mountains and cruel windswept plateaux which exceed 10,000 feet above the Great Ice Barrier, and are probably colder even than the Yakutsk district in Siberia where the thermometer has recorded 93°

below zero. Anyway Rear-Admiral Byrd observed a mid-winter temperature on the Great Ice Barrier of 85° when only a few hundred feet above sea level ; what the thermometer then stood at on that South Polar plateau, 10° farther south in latitude and at an altitude of more than 10,000 feet greater—I shiver to think.

Now look at Shackleton's, Amundsen's and Scott's South Polar sledge tracks and look at the track charts of Hubert Wilkins, Lincoln Ellsworth and Byrd, and turn up their meteorological records in the summer. No one has been on those cruel windswept plateaux in the Antarctic mid-winter so far, and until the South Polar plateau has been visited by man, or its mid-winter temperature taken by a self-recording thermometer, I shall put my money on the Antarctic inland plateau as the coldest part of the Universe. This is, of course, excluding the summits of mountains like Erebus, Discovery, Markham and the 15,000-foot Mount Nansen.

Turn to the lowlands, the barriers where mid-winter and spring journeys have been carried out. Dr. E. A. Wilson's sledge trip from Cape Evans to Cape Crozier across the Great Ice Barrier to study the embryology of the Emperor penguins gave him 77° below zero, although the party was only a few miles from the sea.

And even in spring-sledging my little three-man team experienced 73° below. So even the Antarctic lowlands and barrier surfaces take a good deal of beating !

When, last year, I revisited Australia I had some talks with my fellow sailor-explorers of the Antarctic, and the subject of low temperatures was frequently broached. Discussion led to comparison and I began to believe that Mawson's men had had the worst of the Antarctic climate, this in spite of the fact that Scott's men and Shackleton's men had wintered more than ten degrees farther south.

On May 14, 1912, in the eastern part of Adélie Land the anemometer recorded an average of over 90 miles per hour for the twenty-four hours, and on that day, at times, the gale blew with a speed of over *100 m.p.h.* for a full hour several times. For a whole fortnight that May the average never fell below 70 m.p.h. !

Search through a score of books about Antarctica; only one that I have read gives a vivid picture of this pitiless cold—C. F. Laseron's *South With Mawson.* Dr. L. M. Gould, an outstanding geologist in Byrd's American aeronautical expedition 1929–30, has given the most appropriate title to his own very valuable work, published in 1931. He calls the book *Cold.*

Yes, that should be the name for this little introductory chapter, COLD, COLD, COLD.

The first party to spend the complete winter in Antarctica, 1898–99, was that on board the *Belgica* under the leadership of Lieutenant Adrien de Gerlache, Royal Belgian Navy, and during this unintentional winter, drifting about beset with heavy pack ice, the little *Belgica's* staff recorded a thermometer reading of 45° below zero—when the mercury froze ! This, their lowest recorded temperature, was on September 8, 1898, when the ship was as far as 70° S. latitude.

Fifty years ago, at Cape Adare, Louis Bernacchi, physicist and meteorologist of the Southern Cross expedition, obtained some interesting facts about the Antarctic climate; in fact from February 1899 until January 1900 he kept a full meteorological record and gave − 43·1° as the coldest temperature recorded (August 4, 1899).

During August, the coldest month, the mean temperature was − 13·4° Fahrenheit.

The Southern Cross expedition was the first to winter on shore in the Antarctic. The landing party occupied a fairly comfortable hut and were well provided with clothing, much better than that of the crew of the *Belgica* whose plans did not include wintering as far into the Antarctic as 71° S.

It was my fellow *Worcester* cadet Gerald Doorly, who served in the two relief expeditions of 1902–03–04 to search out and set free Captain Scott's *Discovery*, who wrote the music to J. D. Morrison's song *The Ice King*. Morrison was our Chief Engineer when in March 1903 the 147-foot whaler *Morning* turned her tiny bowsprit northward and away from the besetting ice that held Scott and his men prisoners for another long cold polar night.

The song begins :

Down in the deadly stillness, cut off from the world—alone
Held in the grasp of the Ice King, on the steps of his crystal
    throne :
Waiting returning sunshine, waiting the help we'll bring—
Wearily watching the hours go by, till the *Morning* comes
    with the spring.

and ends with the refrain :

Far away in that cold white land,
In the home of the Great Ice King !
Braving his fury—daring his wrath,
When honour and glory are showing the path ;
God will keep them from harm and scathe—
Till the *Morning* comes with the spring.

Chapter Two

THE EARLIEST VISITORS

To Hugh Robert Mill and to J. Gordon Hayes, British Antarctic explorers, as well as those of France, the United States, Russia, Germany, Norway, Sweden, the Argentine, Scotland, Japan and, of course, Australia, owe a great debt for their histories of Antarctic exploration.

The Siege of the South Pole by H. R. Mill and *The Conquest of the South Pole* by J. Gordon Hayes are full of information about the desolate Antarctic, just, clear and true. Both authors are enthusiasts in love with their subject, both able to appreciate the successes and short-comings of those whose endeavours have made that Siege and Conquest possible.

Then there is another monumental work, *Fangst og Forskning i Sydishavet*, in the language of the modern Vikings, by Bjarne Aagaard. These three might in my lifetime be called " the Antarctic Explorers' and South Sea Whalers' Bible ".

The three books mentioned do, most certainly, take into consideration the little-navigated waters lying between 60° S. and the Antarctic Circle itself, and in the most comprehensive chronological lists of Antarctic voyages from 1700 to 1930 the same scheme has been adopted. Even the elusive Bouvet Island, which is in 54° 26' S. and 3° 24' E., turns up again and again. I have seen Bouvet from ship and boat, and collected terns, silver-grey petrels, brown-backed petrels and storm petrels from its surf-beaten shores, but even that world-famous navigator, Captain James Cook, failed to find it in 1775 and Captain Sir James Clark Ross, one of the

Dii Majores of Polar exploration, after his last Antarctic voyage in 1843 was bitterly disappointed in his failure " to locate that child of the mist, Bouvet Island ". Whether the weather was too misty to see properly or abnormal refraction and/or an erroneous rate had been used for Cook's and Ross's chronometers we cannot say, but the fact remains that Bouvet beat both !

And now for the Early Visitors !

I suppose the seals and penguins were the first to land on the Antarctic Continent, although giant petrels and skua gulls may have come out of the Ark simultaneously and formed, as it were, a " bomber and fighter escort ", but these creatures keep no records, and therefore we must take the circumnavigatory voyages and the expeditions to the Southern Seas of the British seamen Cook and Ross, Bellingshausen the Russian, the American Wilkes, the Frenchman Dumont d'Urville, and the many intrepid sealers and venturers, mostly British and American, supported by Norwegian, Belgian, Swedish and German, who in the nineteenth century carried out the pioneer work of exploring the hitherto neglected and desolate Antarctic.

Before the nineteenth century, Captain James Cook, a Yorkshireman, made his famous voyage towards the South Pole and round the world with H.M.S. *Resolution* and *Adventure* in the years 1772–75, and, on a memorable day for all British Antarctic explorers, January 17, 1773, he crossed the Antarctic Circle, where no man so far had ventured. Exactly one hundred and thirty-nine years later Captain Robert Falcon Scott reached the South Pole, a month after the valiant Norseman, Roald Amundsen, had done so.

Cook remained a very short time south of the Antarctic Circle, but returned in January 1774 and forced his way as far as 71° 10′ S., 106° 54′ W. when he met with ice conditions, "thick fogs, snowstorms, intense cold and every other thing that can render navigation dangerous . . ."

Cook described the desolate Antarctic as " a country doomed by nature never once to feel the warmth of the sun's rays, but to lie buried in everlasting snow and ice ".

His remark " beneath those great ice-cliffs there no doubt lay land, but of what use was land that wore as a breastplate half a mile of ice ? " expressed a wealth of common sense.

For another fifty years the Antarctic was left in her loneland silence and then the adventurous Russian, Fabian Gottlieb von Bellingshausen, with the *Wostok* under his own command and the *Mirny* under Lazarev, sailed from Kronstadt in 1819 under orders from Czar Alexander I to push as far south as possible.

Sailing round the southern side of South Georgia and plotting its coastline as accurately as this running survey permitted, Bellingshausen then made for South Sandwich Islands and discovered the Traversey Islands, on one of which, Sawadowskji, was an active volcano. Early in January 1820 Bellingshausen reached the Sandwich group and charted them, after which he sailed southwards, being held up frequently by ice, both pack and barrier. However, he reached latitude 69° 21' S. in longitude 2° 15' W, and after various attempts got almost as far south again, on February 17–18, when he was stopped by " an interminable rampart of ice extending east and west as far as the eye could see ".

Bellingshausen wintered in Sydney, New South Wales, and then sailed south again on December 1, 1820, in longitude approximately 164° E. where in latitude 62° 18' S. he met with icebergs and pack-ice ; one berg was nearly seven miles in length.

Bellingshausen again crossed the Antarctic Circle, in fact he crossed it many times, and reached latitude 69° 53' S. in longitude 92° 19' W. on January 22, 1821.

In latitude 68° 57' S., longitude 90° 46' W. a steep lofty island was sighted, estimated as having an altitude of 4,000 feet. This island was christened Peter I Island.

As Bellingshausen was convinced that more land was to be found in this region, he steered to the eastward in latitude 68° 30′ S., and a week later sighted the Antarctic Continent itself, in the position now named Alexander I Land, and thus to Fabian Gottlieb von Bellingshausen and Captain Lazarev, and the Imperial Russian Navy, belongs the honour of first sighting and charting land within the Antarctic Circle !

Bellingshausen's Antarctic voyage coincided with the visit of James Weddell, the enterprising seal-hunter, and of Walker, Powell, Palmer and Pendleton, Brisbane and others to the high southern latitude in the neighbourhood of the South Orkneys and South Shetlands.

The dangerous waters of the Antarctic Ocean to the east of Graham Land have been named after the redoubtable Weddell, who penetrated as far as 74° 15′ S. in longitude 34° 17′ W. in the year 1823.

The invasion of the Antarctic Seas and adjacent waters close northward by sealers opened up, as it were, the way for scientific explorers and wrote a fine chapter in the Story of the Sea. Anyone who has seen the sealing schooners that sailed at 12 and 13 knots to Nova Scotia and elsewhere with their cargoes of sealskins is not likely to forget them nor their captains and mates. Tough, daring and expert, those who manned the schooners were the sort of men that Peary picked for the Arctic, men like the renowned Bob Bartlett, his second-in-command. But these adventurous spirits almost exterminated the seals. Weddell discovered the weighty hair seal, commonest type in Antarctica, which now bears his name, and provides the fresh meat supply popular with most South Polar explorers.

As far back as 1894 I was taken out to the wreck of the Norwegian barque *Ørnen* on the Goodwin Sands by Steve Penny, captain and owner of the Ramsgate lugger *Champion*, and there I kept a tally of 1,176 Weddell sealskins brought home from the South Shetlands via the Falkland Islands. The lugger's crew thought that they had made their fortunes, but the total salvage only amounted to £1,500, and the net sum, after legal and other expenses had been deducted, left little more than the price of a " couple of pints all round "—my reward being a bottle of lemonade and a few slices of polony sausage. However, more about seals anon.

After Weddell followed Captain John Biscoe in 1830, the discoverer of Enderby Land, named after the public-spirited Enderby Bros., shipowners, who encouraged their captains besides trading to investigate, chart and explore. Biscoe landed on Adelaide Island in 67° 15′ S., 68° 28′ W., and Captain John Balleny, another great sailor, managed to combine exploration with trade and add to our Antarctic knowledge. A whole group of islands to the N.N.W. of South Victoria Land were named after him. On one of these islands, discovered by Balleny, is a magnificent ice-capped mountain named after his second-in-command, Freeman's Peak. It was probably this lofty cone on Young Island that Lieutenant Pennell, while in command of Scott's *Terra Nova* in March 1912, went into such raptures about. To my great sorrow I did not see the Balleny Islands as, although on board the ship, I was lying in the captain's bunk, paralysed with scurvy and terribly close to death's door.

There is an active volcano on Buckle Island, another of the Balleny Group.

Captain Freeman of the diminutive *Sabrina* was lost with his 54-ton cutter and all hands somewhere about March 24, 1840, and with the Enderby Bros.' Captains' discoveries unfolds the true nature of the Antarctic—cruel, stormy, desolate and merciless.

And now appear the *Erebus* and *Terror* whose commanders Ross and Crozier properly drew aside the curtain that had hidden that continent of ice barrier and plateau and glacier and mountain range for thousands, nay, millions of years.

But, before turning the searchlight on to the voyages of discovery and research in the Antarctic of Captain Sir James Clark Ross, R.N., during the years 1839-43, it seems appropriate to give some account of the work of the French naval explorer, Dumont d'Urville, and of that distinguished and scientific United States Naval Lieutenant, Charles Wilkes.

Unfortunately, and perhaps unfairly, the work of d'Urville and Wilkes has been subjected to a good deal of adverse criticism in the past, but when one considers that the whole of their exploration was carried out well over a century ago entirely under sail, with somewhat primitive instruments for navigational, astronomical, magnetic, hydrographical and meteorological observations, and when one realizes the appalling weather conditions faced by themselves and their followers, much of the criticism appears trivial, often it is prejudiced and occasionally quite unfair.

Captain Jules Sebastien Cesar Dumont d'Urville of the French Navy left France in 1837 with two ships— the *Astrolabe*, which he himself commanded, and the *Zélée*, Captain Jacquinot. Sailing via Magellan Straits, which he spent some time surveying, to the Pacific Antarctic area near Graham Land, d'Urville encountered the pack-ice on January 22, 1838 in 69° 39′ S. and 44° 47′ W.

Here the pack appeared too heavy to force, and after hovering about for nearly two months between the ice and the South Orkney Islands, when his ships were to the south-west of the South Shetlands, land was sighted in approximately 63° S.—evidently the same land as that which was sighted by Palmer and Biscoe. However, d'Urville christened part of it after the reigning monarch, Louis Philippe Land, and gave names to the highest mountains seen, calling them after the two captains of the *Astrolabe* and the *Zélée*. In the beginning of March d'Urville left the icy waters of the Antarctic and carried out exploratory work in the Pacific, as he had originally intended. We must not mix up d'Urville's first Antarctic incursion with his anthropological expedition in Oceania. The Pacific, not the Antarctic, was the Frenchman's Happy Hunting Ground, and it was in the Pacific that the *Astrolabe* and *Zélée* spent the best part of two years of their truly famous voyage.

However, in excess of his instructions from the Ministry of Marine, d'Urville, urged perhaps by the successes of Ross and Wilkes, once more sailed southward between 120° and 160° E. He left Hobart on New Year's Day, 1840, and met the first ice in 60° S. Continuing southward, he met with a number of gigantic tabular bergs or ice islands in 64°.

On January 20, in latitude 66°, preparations were made for receiving " Father Antarctic " on board, and there was great hilarity. Nevertheless, the actual crossing of the Antarctic Circle was delayed by meeting ice-covered land in 66° 30′ S, 138° E., which ran east and west, and which d'Urville named Adélie Land. A chain of small rocky islets served to hoist the Tricolour on, and for purposes of annexation for La Belle France.

Magnetic observers were landed on an iceberg and a dip of 86° was recorded. The only live specimens taken were what are now known as Adélie Penguins, and when killed their crops were found to contain small pieces of granite of various colours.

For a couple of days the two ships sailed slowly to the eastward, determining the height of the glaciated land to run up to 1,500 feet.

In longitude 135° 30′ E. the edge of the besetting pack was found to trend due north and to stop further eastward progress.

On January 24, whilst the ships were working their

way to the northward between a fleet of tabular bergs, they were struck by a sudden gale and separated. Both ships suffered severely but escaped collision with the formidable bergs, and fortunately sighted one another on the following day.

More bad weather, and more damage, then thick weather and a great surprise on January 29 when a strange sail—a brig flying the American colours—was sighted.

Strangely enough no signals were exchanged! The brig was soon lost in the fog and that was the end of the story—or should have been.

On January 30, in 64° 30′ S. and 131° E., when steering to the westward, a wall of ice over a hundred feet in height was seen to the southward, and soundings showed no bottom in two hundred fathoms.

D'Urville, considering that this was similar glaciated land, or ice barrier, to Adélie Land (which he had named after his wife), named this new discovery Côte Clarie, after Madame Jacquinot. Meeting with more heavy pack farther to the westward and losing sight of the Côte Clarie barrier, d'Urville withdrew from the South Polar Seas on February 1, 1840.

His voluminous accounts are in picturesque and somewhat flowery language, but the sketches, the best of which were by the artist Goupil, added greatly to the value of d'Urville's accounts of his Antarctic ventures.

What a pity it seems that Lieutenant Charles Wilkes and Dumont d'Urville did not meet and dine together in the matey fashion of sailors before they went a-sailing into the icebound Southern Seas! They might have co-operated splendidly instead of seeing one another momentarily in the fog.

I used to read in French about the work of the *Astrolabe* and *Zélée* when I was working up for my entrance exams for the Navy and as an acting sub-lieutenant, and

Ernest Pelluet (my French master and afterwards my farmer-partner in Forest Edge Farm, Athabasca Landing, Alberta) called his daughter " Zélée " after the beautiful corvette with such a fine record of service in the Sapphire Seas of the Pacific and the Emerald Seas of Antarctica.

Dr. Jean Charcot, the French polar explorer and contemporary of Scott, was an ardent admirer of Admiral Dumont d'Urville (as he afterwards became), and so evidently is Hugh Robert Mill, who tells that when d'Urville was in his 'teens, on seeing an old Greek statue recently unearthed, he wrote home in terms of such rapturous appreciation of its beauty that an order was sent to secure the statue for the Louvre at any cost. There is something very attractive and yet very touching about this artistic French sailor's career. He frequently suffered ill-health and was a martyr to gout ; in fact one day when he hobbled down to his ship just before sailing to the Far South, one of his matelots was heard to say " Oh, that old bloke won't lead us very far " (*Oh, ce bonhomme-la ne nous mènera pas loin !*). All the same, d'Urville took his crews a great deal farther than any of them cared to go in those days of heavily-sparred, old-fashioned sailing ships.

The " rival " Wilkes, with Lieutenant Hudson as his second-in-command, was appointed to lead the motley squadron which sailed from the United States in late summer of 1838 and which consisted of the following ships :

Vincennes
    780-ton sloop-of-war, commander Lt. Chas. Wilkes
Peacock
    650-ton sloop-of-war   ,,   Lt. Wm. Hudson
Porpoise
    230-ton gun brig   ,,   Lt. Cadwalader Ringgold

Sea Gull
    110-ton Old New York commander Passed-Midship-
       Pilot Boat   man J. W. E. Reid

Flying Fish
    96-ton Pilot Boat   ,,   Mr. Samuel R. Knox

Relief
    Store Ship   ,,   Lt. A. K. Long
    (sent home early on as quite unsuitable on account
    of her slow speed and general unwieldiness).

The total crews comprised 83 officers, 12 scientists, artists and civilian staff, and a crew of 345 men. Of these only 221 returned to the U.S. with the expedition, or were sent home in American vessels. Of the remainder 62 were discharged abroad, 47 deserted, and 15 died or were drowned. This meant many changes, and of the 585 engaged altogether, there were in all 127 desertions !

Poor Wilkes, his burdens must have been well-nigh intolerable, yet he saw the business through in spite of setbacks and reverses as serious as losing the *Sea Gull* with all hands early in the voyage.

For sheer hardship and hazard outstripping anything in the history of actual voyages in Antarctic seas, I can imagine nothing to compare with Charles Wilkes' narrative of the American Exploring Expedition in the years 1838–42, with the one exception of Shackleton's glory-covered open-boat journey in the *James Caird* (April–May 1916).

The Siege of the South Pole gives enough of Wilkes' and his men's experiences to make all adventurous spirits raise their hats in salute !

In the year 1900 Dr. Karl Fricker's book, *The Antarctic Regions*, was published in English. Fricker, like H. R. Mill, has quite a lot to say about Wilkes, and gives him credit for " discovering the longest coastline " yet seen in the Antarctic Regions. It extends from 97° E. to 164° E. longitude, and comprises Termination Land,

Knox Land, Budd Land, Totten Land, Sabrina Land, North Land, Clarie and Adélie Lands, Point Case, Point Emmons, Peacock Bay, Reynold's Peak, Eld Peak and Ringgold's Knoll.

All of the foregoing are situated just without or just within the South Polar Circle, and whether accurately charted or not, they do, combined with d'Urville's, Balleny's, Biscoe's, Weddell's and Bellingshausen's discoveries, give the first rough outline of the Antarctic Terra Nova.

And mighty cold outlines they were too, ice-cliffs, a few steep, virtually inaccessible islands like the Ballenys, sentinels to that cruel desolate continent—that does not contain a single tree or edible plant or pasture —and some outstanding mountain peaks, a few volcanoes and occasional rocky outcrops.

In the accounts of the old Antarctic explorers' voyages there are mostly descriptions of those dread battles with the elements, gales on the edge of the pack. But not only the old Antarctic explorers and the early twentieth-century seamen-adventurers, but the winged explorers like Wilkins, Lincoln Ellsworth and—greatest of all aviator-explorers—Byrd, know what hazards and risks are run in these Antarctic storms.

When youngsters first go to sea they are subjected to a good deal of leg-pulling. One of the things they are adjured to do is to be sure to throw ashes, dirty water, and rubbish to windward in a gale. The simplest first voyager, as a rule, is incredulous and repeats " To windward?—Why to windward ? " and the old salt replies immediately, " Yes, to windward because if you do that once, you'll never do it again."

And so in the pack-ice. Once snug in the pack and protected by a field of floes only the merest tyro will work the ship free when a gale is blowing. I saw the Chief Officer in my first Antarctic voyage deliberately work the little relief ship *Morning* out of the ice to face a gale on the edge of the pack. That gale developed into a storm and then into a hurricane which was far more than an icy nightmare—the farther we were blown out of the compact mass of grinding floes the worse it became for us. A ship drifts to leeward far more rapidly than an iceberg, or an ice floe, with so much of its bulk below the surface.

Poor little *Morning*! She crashed on to the weather side of the larger floes and the light stuff crashed on to her—lumps weighing a ton or two were thrown on to her decks and broke the light bulwarks besides damaging the deck-fittings and, as the sea became worse and the waves increased in size, sheets of spray were driven on board to turn almost instantly into solid ice, which hampered the decks and hatches. This went on for three days and our weak-powered engines would scarcely keep the ship's head up to the wind. We had to set a strong tarpaulin in the weather mizzen rigging to help us as no sail whatever could be set.

All hands remained ready for any emergency, clothed, sea-booted and protected by oilskins on top of their cold-weather clothing. The look-outs were doubled and perched in the eyes of the ship and had to be relieved every half-hour to prevent them from becoming frost-bitten. Yes, I remember that gale which developed into a three-day hurricane. Sometimes the driving snow would make it impossible to see a yard, it was most painful to the eyes. Squalls, unbelievably fierce, would strike the ship and heel her over until we thought she must capsize. And then more great lumps of ice would hit the ship with sickening thuds, and much of it would come on board. Fortunately, a good deal of it went over the side to leeward. Whatever any of our little crew may say, we were all of us thoroughly frightened.

We certainly had auxiliary engines and handy double topsails, but Wilkes and Ross and d'Urville and others had no steam power, and had to do everything under their own ungainly great square topsails which carried three and even four reefs, in the early explorers' days.

But, even in the late forties of this century with high-powered steamships or motor vessels, the Antarctic is full of heavy ice which might sink any ship ever built or ever likely to be built.

The modern Antarctic explorer has many advantages over his predecessors. One of the greatest, of course, is wireless, either for communication or for entertainment. In my first Admiral's command I was able to receive and send wireless messages, and live again my Antarctic days with the silence of the desolate Antarctic frequently broken, which was a new and refreshing experience.

Chapter Three

ROSS

WHENEVER I pass through Aylesbury my thoughts turn to the story of the *Erebus* and *Terror* and their astounding voyage of adventure and scientific research to the Antarctic Regions, during the years 1839–43, for it was at Aston House, Aylesbury, that Ross wrote the story of this great enterprise.

Captain Sir James Clark Ross, to whom the Command of the Expedition was given, was already well known as an arctic explorer, who had, under Captain Parry, located the North Magnetic Pole, and acquired considerable knowledge of polar travelling and ice navigation. His first polar experience had been gained at nineteen and by the age of thirty he was a seasoned arctic explorer. Ross was appointed to command H.M.S. *Erebus* while his trusty and tried friend and messmate, Commander F. R. M. Crozier, was given the command of H.M.S. *Terror*. Each ship carried a complement of 64 officers and men.

This expedition was easily the best that had ever left our shores. Outfit and equipment, provisions and stores were the finest that money in those days could buy, and a glance at Ross's introductory remarks (which fill nearly fifty pages and run into close on twelve thousand words) gives a good idea of the thoroughness with which this British Antarctic expedition was organized and launched.

The " circumnavigation of the Antarctic Pole " was only one of the many general and scientific objects of the expedition, and the comparatively few living people who have read Sir James Ross's *Voyage to the Southern Seas* realize what a wonderful record and narrative it is, and all this before the invention of the typewriter !

Compare Ross's expedition with that of Wilkes from the organization and fitting-out viewpoint—and you will revolt a good deal against the injustice and uncharitableness of Wilkes's critics.

However, this is not a discussion group report on Antarctic exploration as it was conducted in the 1840's ; it is intended to be a story of the difficulties of South Polar exploration, how they were surmounted and how the physical features (or physiography) have been pieced together and thrown on the screen until this desolate continent has come to be used for a " cold-war " training and exercising ground on a very vast scale.

The two ships *Erebus* and *Terror* were specially strengthened barque-rigged bomb-throwing vessels of 370 and 340 tons. They left Chatham on September 25, 1839, to circumnavigate the Antarctic Pole, as stated, and also to carry out an ambitious magnetic survey on a genuinely scientific expedition.

Sailing via the Cape of Good Hope to Kerguelen, that and other sub-Antarctic islands were visited and scientific observations made. Ross then came to Hobart, Tasmania (or Van Diemens Land) where he established a magnetic observatory and was well looked after by the Governor, Sir John Franklin, the Arctic explorer. He sailed southwards on November 12, 1840, and sighted his first iceberg in 63° 20′ S., and soon afterwards the two ships passed a chain of bergs, some of great size and height. Ross was surprised at their uniformity of shape ; he called them " tabular " icebergs, and noted their perpendicular cliffs, and their " lack of colour and variety of form ", which distinguished them from the beautiful Arctic bergs.

By December 29 he was sighting whales in great numbers, black whales, hunch-backs, sperms and rorquals.

The first week of the year 1841 found the two ships in the pack ice and Ross learnt of its great extent, variety and nature. His splendid leadership inspired his staff to make first-class records of all that they observed, and what with new species of birds, skua gulls, dainty white ice petrels, brown-backed and little black petrels, and clumsy giant petrels who ate so much that they could not always " take off " from the ice fields, the zoologists soon had their note-books filled.

And then came the seals and penguins. New species were discovered, and a rare seal with a goitre-like neck was found and named after Ross himself. But all this interest in animal life and crustaceans and fish and pack-ice faded into insignificance when the high mountains of a new land were shown towering in a magnificent panorama of glistening white and blue.

Ross named this great white ice-bound land " Victoria Land " after his young sovereign. The wonderland of mountain ranges and the mighty and majestic peaks had names bestowed upon them, like Admiralty Range, Mount Minto, Mount Sabine and Mount Herschell, after important ministers, scientists and leading peers of the day. The capes and bays, islands and seas were reserved for the lesser luminaries, like Cape Crozier, Cape Bird, Wood Bay, McMurdo Bay (Sound) and so forth. The *pièce de résistance*, Ross Island, he named after himself, and the two volcanoes, one 13,500 and the other 10,000 feet in altitude, he christened Mounts Erebus and Terror.

Ross charted Victoria Land accurately enough, and his men landed on the Possession Islands. He discovered what will always be one of the world's greatest wonders, the Great Ice Barrier, that frozen Sahara which we now know to extend for five hundred miles and more southward. He sailed almost four hundred miles eastward along it, and named that also, the Ross Ice Barrier.

The *Erebus* and *Terror* worked eastward as far as 160° W. longitude, charting the barrier cliff for almost the whole of its length, taking deep sea soundings and magnetic and hydrographic observations and industriously recording everything seen, and giving thereby such a true picture of Victoria Land, Coulman Island, Franklin Island, Beaufort Island, the Great Ice Barrier, and the ice conditions of the Ross Sea, that Ross's first Antarctic voyage gave later explorers an " Open Sesame " to Antarctica's heart.

What his sailors must have endured, trimming yards as the two ships manœuvred mostly under full sail, one can scarcely imagine, and when recounting how on April 6 Ross returned to Tasmania's beautiful River Derwent and was again greeted by Sir John Franklin, it is befitting to set down his words : ". . . to call forth our gratitude to God for His guidance and preservation during the arduous and hazardous operations in which we have been engaged".

After refitting in Tasmania, Ross sailed south again at the end of 1841 and continued his glorious work. On March 13, 1842, in one of those terrible gales that South Polar explorers all know, the ships passed through a chain of bergs under such hazardous circumstances that the greatest writer of tempestuous sea lore would have difficulty in describing what the two ships endured —sails torn from the bolt-ropes, sheets of icy water crashing on to their decks, topsails in holes, and cool bravery which can never have been exceeded. The ships collided, the *Erebus* lost her bowsprit and presented a woeful spectacle with her broken spars and damaged rigging.

After much dangerous sailing in the Antarctic when their farthest south latitude 78° 10' was reached, and the Barrier farther explored, Ross headed northward and eastward, and finally anchored in Port Louis, East Falkland Island, where he hauled up his ships to repair them, and then in lower latitudes and warmer seas he completed his magnificent scientific voyaging and made his way back to the shores of Old England, which were sighted on December 2, 1843, after four years' absence.

Ross succeeded in locating the South Magnetic Pole in 75° 5′ S. and longitude 154° 8′ E. and certainly repaid the country in full for the cost of his expedition. He ranks as one of our greatest scientific seamen-explorers.

Sir James Ross's *Voyage to the Southern Seas* contains indeed some remarkable and truly exciting illustrations, besides maps and wood-cuts, which make the two volumes, published by John Murray in 1847, an outstanding work apart from the English used, its naval phraseology and the rich and exciting narrative of Britain's first Naval Antarctic expedition.

In this book is a classic saga of a gale and collision which ranks high, very high, in South Polar literature, and one which should certainly find its place in this story of the desolate Antarctic. It runs :

March 12, 1842. In the evening the wind increased so much and the snow showers became so incessant that we were obliged to proceed under more moderate sail. Numerous small pieces of ice were also met with, warning us of the presence of bergs, concealed by the thickly falling snow : before midnight I directed the topsails to be close-reefed and every arrangement made for rounding to until daylight, deeming it too hazardous to run any longer : our people had hardly completed these operations when a large berg was seen ahead, and quite close to us : the ship was immediately hauled to wind on the port tack, with the expectation of being able to weather it, but just at this moment the *Terror* was observed running down upon us under her top-sails and foresail ; and as it was impossible for her to clear both the berg and the *Erebus* collision was inevitable. We instantly hove all aback to diminish the violence of the shock ; but the concussion when she struck us was such as to throw almost everyone off his feet ; our bowsprit, fore-topmast and other smaller spars were carried away ; and the ships hanging together, entangled by their rigging and dashing against each other with fearful violence were falling down upon the weather face of the lofty berg under our lee, against which the waves were breaking and foaming to near the summit of its perpendicular cliffs. Sometimes she rose high above us, almost exposing her keel to view, and again descended as we in our turn rose to the top of the wave, threatening to bury her beneath us, whilst the crashing of the breaking upperworks and boats increased the horror of the scene. Providentially they gradually forged past each other, and separated before we drifted down amongst the foaming breakers, and we had the gratification of seeing her clear the end of the berg and of feeling that she was safe. But she left us completely disabled ; the wrecks of the spars so encumbered the lower yards, that we were unable to make sail, so as to get head-way on the ship ; nor had we room to wear round, being by this time so close to the berg that the waves, when they struck against it, threw back their sprays into our ship. The only way left to us to extricate ourselves from this awful and appalling situation was by resorting to the hazardous expedient of a stern-board, which nothing could justify during such a gale and with so high a sea running, but to avert the danger which every moment threatened us of being dashed to pieces. The heavy rolling of the vessel, and the probability of the masts giving way each time the lower yard-arms struck against the cliffs, which were towering high above our mastheads, rendered it a service of extreme danger to loose the main-sail ; but no sooner was the order given than the daring spirit of the British seaman manifested itself—the men ran up the rigging with as much alacrity as on any ordinary occasion ; and although more than once driven off the yard, they after a short time succeeded in loosing the sail. Amidst the roar of the wind and sea, it was difficult both to hear and to execute the orders that were given, so that it was three-quarters of an hour before we could get the yard braced bye, and the maintack hauled on board sharp aback—an expedient that perhaps had never before been resorted to by seamen in such weather : but it had the desired effect ; the ship gathered stern-way, plunging her stern into the sea, washing away the gig and quarter boats, and with her lower yard-arms scraping the rugged base of the berg, we in a few minutes reached its western termination ; the " under tow ", as it is called, or the reaction of the water from its vertical cliffs, alone preventing us being driven to atoms against it. No sooner had we cleared it, than another was seen directly astern of us, against which we were running ; and the difficulty now was to get the ship's head turned round and pointed fairly through between the two bergs, the breadth of the intervening space not exceeding three times her own breadth ; this, however, we happily accomplished ; and in a few minutes, after getting before the wind, she dashed through the narrow channel, between two perpendicular walls of ice, and the foaming breakers which stretched across it, and the next moment we were in smooth water under its lee.

The *Terror's* light was immediately seen and answered ; she had rounded to, waiting for us, and the painful state of suspense her people must have endured as to our fate could not have been much less than our own ; for the necessity of constant and energetic action to meet the momentarily varying circumstances of our situation, left us no time to reflect on our imminent danger.

We hove to on the port tack, under the lee of the berg, which now afforded us invaluable protection from the fury of the storm, which was still raging above and around us ; and commenced clearing away the wreck of the broken spars, saving as much of the rigging as possible, whilst a party were engaged preparing others to replace them.

As soon as day broke we had the gratification of learning that the *Terror* had only lost two or three small spars and had not suffered any serious damage ; the signal of " all's well " which we hoisted before there was light enough for them to see it, and kept flying until it was answered, served to relieve their minds as speedily as possible of any remaining anxiety on our account.

A cluster of bergs was seen to windward extending as far as the eye could discern, and so closely connected, that,

25

except the small opening by which we had escaped, they appeared to form an unbroken continuous line ; it seems, therefore, not at all improbable that the collision with the *Terror* was the means of our preservation, by forcing us backwards to the only practicable channel, instead of permitting us, as we were endeavouring, to run to the eastwards, and become entangled in a labyrinth of heavy bergs from which escape might have been impracticable, or perhaps impossible.

And so it goes on, this narrative, turning from gale and collision in the pack-ice or completely surrounded by bergs to " obtaining numerous magnetic observations . . . which will enable philosophers to determine whether, as in the Northern Magnetic latitudes, there be two foci of greater magnetic intensity, or whether it be not confined to one spot in the Antarctic regions and that not very distant from the Southern Magnetic Pole. . . ."

Truly Ross personifies " the Englishman with his customary sang-froid ".

Chapter Four

WHALES, SEALS AND PENGUINS

Whales and Antarctic Whaling. Among the copious reports from Ross and others who had made their way into the Antarctic Seas, came accounts of Antarctic cetacea or whales, and the whalers of the nineteenth century, finding that the Arctic whaling industry was showing signs of exhaustion, turned their attention to the Antarctic, and with the introduction of steam began to develop what to-day is an extremely profitable industry.

In 1892–93 Dr. W. S. Bruce, the Scottish marine biologist, who embarked in the Dundee whaler *Balaena*, and Dr. Donald on board the *Active*, together with Captain Larsen of the Norwegian whaling steamer *Jason*, visited Elephant Island, the South Orkneys, and in Larsen's case pushed southward well into the Weddell Sea. Larsen, on December 1, 1893, discovered new land in 66° S. and approximately 60° W. which he named King Oscar II Land, besides which he landed on one of a chain of islands, Christensen Volcano. But the whales met with were not the right whales, but rorquals or finners, and the visit of Dundee whalers in 1892–93, and that of the *Antarctic* a couple of years later, ended in disappointment.

The captains of the whalers had to content themselves with loading up with seals of which there were, and probably still are, great numbers. The whaling industry in the twentieth century has mostly passed into the hands of the Norwegians, who now employ huge cookery ships in which they dispose of the carcases in the most scientific way so that almost every portion of the whale is utilized—oil, flesh, ambergris and bone; and the flotillas of small whalers mounting harpoon guns are manned by the best-paid mariners or fishermen afloat.

A good deal of anxiety is being shown nowadays by Norwegian and Australian whaling crews at the activity of the Japanese in the Antarctic whaling industry, and at the beginning of February 1949 I listened, in a Norwegian ship, to a discussion on this subject in which it was stated that the Japs were employing radar to locate the unfortunate cetacea and then killing them with depth charges.

Black whales, blue whales, white-bellied whales, brown-backed whales, Sibbald's whales, sperm whales, bottle-nosed whales, hump-backed or hunch-backed whales, and killer whales and very occasionally the Southern Right Whale (*Balaena Australis*) we used to see in 1902–3–4 and 1910–11–12–13, when I performed my Antarctic service as sub-lieutenant, lieutenant and commander before the steam whalers properly invaded the Antarctic Seas and commenced the annihilation of the Southern Cetacea.

In Scott's last expedition Dr. Wilson thought we had found a new species of white-bellied whale with a sabre-like fin, estimated by Captain Scott at four feet in length.

Concerning these Antarctic whales, the Norwegians, Svend Foyn and C. A. Larsen, have done most to commercialize them, Svend Foyn by inventing a gun which was mounted originally in a 40-ton steam vessel and which discharged a harpoon attached to a strong grapnel rope. When the whale is hit the two shanks of the harpoon open and explode a small bomb. The whale's body is hauled back by a steam winch, then secured alongside and inflated and towed to the melting house or cookery ship. As many as six whales at a time have been brought back by one of the little whalers.

Svend Foyn Land, which is right on the Polar Circle,

lies on the eastern side of Graham Land, just southward of King Oscar II Land. It commemorates the old Tönsberg shipbuilder who constructed the strongest wooden whalers ever built. As it is in longitude 62° W. it is probably the *Svend Foyn Island* of the Norwegian chart showing Larsen's, Nordenskjöld's and Wilkins' discoveries of 1893, 1902, 1928, 1930.

Curiously enough the British Graham Land Expedition does not show King Oscar II Land on its Graham Land chart. Unfortunately there have been too many changes in the names and configuration of Graham Land.

Byrd's 1946–47 vast naval Antarctic expedition ignores Graham Land altogether, and in its place appears the name Palmer Peninsula, evidently after the American captain, Nathaniel B. Palmer, who commanded the 40-ton cutter *Hero*, one of five small vessels of a flotilla in the charge of Captain Benjamin Pendleton, which made its headquarters in Yankee Harbour, Deception Island, 63° S., 61° W., for sealing in the Antarctic summer of 1820–21.

Pendleton from the summit of Deception Island observed, one fine day, several mountains far to the southward; one of them was an active volcano. Palmer was sent off to look more closely at the new mountains, and he found them to be part of a great peninsula stretching far away southward, snow-covered or ice-capped. This was indeed the Graham Land we know, but after searching through many accounts of discoveries thereabouts, we find that Bellingshausen named this peninsula " Palmer's Land " after meeting the little *Hero* and inviting her captain on board the *Wostok* frigate and entertaining him.

Captain C. A. Larsen during his second southern voyage in the *Jason* (1893–94) discovered one of the largest islands in the west Antarctic archipelago, Svend Foyn Island or Svend Foyn Land, as it has been variously named, and made other important discoveries reaching

68° 10′ S., 59° 59′ W., whilst his colleague, Captain C. J. Evensen, in the *Hertha*, reached 69° 10′ S., 76° 12′ W. Larsen on his first voyage landed on Seymour Island and next year he went over the ice on ski with Søren Andersen to Robertson Island.

In 1893–95 Svend Foyn's whaler *Antarctic*, in the charge of H. J. Bull, made a voyage to the Ross Sea and thus became the first ship to visit these waters since James Clark Ross's days. Bull, with some of his shipmates, landed at Cape Adare on February 24, 1895, and they were the first men to set foot on the new mainland.

The Scottish Dundee whaler *Fleet* and the Norwegian *Jason* and *Antarctic* voyages founded a new era which in northern climes is known as the "Whaling epoch", which developed the whaling industry to a far greater extent than ever before, so that important scientific expeditions were despatched. Several European and other nations took part in addition to Britons and Norsemen.

The science of marine biology opened the way to extensive developments in modern whaling, which brought many millions of pounds to the countries whose enterprising ship owners invested their thousands in this business.

Names like Sir John Murray, Professor Johan Hjort, Professor Shipley of Cambridge University are associated with the development of modern whaling, and certainly Shipley proved that the wealth of life including enormous quantities of diatoms south of latitude 50° S. made whaling a most promising proposition in the Southern Seas. He was one of the first to answer the question "What is the use of Antarctic exploration?" The *Challenger* and the *Valdivia* expeditions contributed immensely to our knowledge of the mysteries of the deep, and the United States' Fishery Commission steamer *Albatross's* voyage to the Pacific all helped to build up the Antarctic whaling industry, and thanks to international scientific co-operation the outstanding marine biologists pooled their knowledge to the advantage of science and humanity.

Seals. The fur seals, which were of great commercial value, and which used to be very plentiful in the South Shetlands, have virtually been exterminated from Antarctic and sub-Antarctic waters.

The four types of hair seal now found in Antarctic seas are :

>Weddell seal
>Crabeater
>Sea leopard
>Ross seal

and I have put them in order of their frequency. I have counted more than a hundred Weddell and Crabeater seals on the frozen sea from Cape Evans, and from aloft in the pack-ice one frequently had thirty to forty in sight. Sea leopards are comparatively rare and the " goitre-necked " Ross seal is very rare. Scott's ubiquitous camera and cinematograph artist, H. G. Ponting, was most successful in filming Weddell and Crabeater seals, getting " close-ups " and " nursery " scenes and indeed making what has now been converted into the sound film *Ninety Degrees South.* Ponting's original film was made as long ago as 1910–11. It gave very special attention to seals, penguins and bird life in the Great White South. Ponting had such imagination that it is no exaggeration to say that he got the seals and penguins to pose for his movie and still pictures. Frank Hurley, Shackleton's able and expert photographer, added greatly to the Antarctic art gallery, as did most of the twentieth-century Antarctic photographers, particularly those of the British Commonwealth and American expeditions. The richer the expedition usually the better the film and photographic results.

When in 1830, or thereabouts, the fur seal was more

or less exterminated, photography was in the embryo stage, and it was not until the twentieth century, or at any rate the end of the nineteenth, that really good animal and bird pictures began to arrive from Antarctica.

To return to the Antarctic seals, in John Rymill's official account of the British Graham Land Expedition of 1934–37 opinion is expressed that the Crabeater seal is best eating and the Weddell seal more fit for dog meat. However, in another part of his book, Weddell seal is described as looking and tasting like veal, a statement with which Scott's men agreed. All of us enjoyed seal liver, and none of us ever could stomach the slightest taste of seal blubber, or penguin fat or blubber either.

In the second Antarctic relief expedition in McMurdo Sound, at the end of January 1904, Dr. Wilson, strolling over to the North beach at Cape Royds, saw what he first took for a prodigiously large seal lying there asleep, but on getting closer to it he perceived that it was quite different from anything in the seal family that he had ever come across. Doorly and I from the *Morning* were both with Wilson at the time, and amongst us we managed to slay the strange-looking giant seal. It proved to be a sea elephant of the species found at Macquarie Island and other sub-Antarctic islands. There are plenty of elephant seals in South Georgia, clumsy-looking brutes, of which Rymill has some very good pictures, perhaps the best of any Antarctic explorer; however, I think for variety and number the late Herbert G. Ponting comes out *facile princeps* for Weddells, Crabeaters, mothers and calves.

In the first Antarctic relief expedition I managed to shoot a sea leopard 11 feet 9 inches in length. The sea leopard is very well named, having more spots on its body than any other Antarctic seal. Racovitzi, the Polish naturalist of the *Belgica*, who has a flair for describing the colour of Antarctic seals and birds, says that the sea leopard's coat is " *gris foncé, moucheté de taches jaunes* ".

Certainly the sea leopard is an elongated weird-looking beast. Dr. Bruce, the Scottish naturalist explorer, measured one fully 13 feet in length. He says that the female is bigger than the male, and states that the sailors nicknamed them serpent seals on account of their lithe, slender bodies and rather snakelike heads.

Borchgrevinck's Southern Cross Expedition gave us a lot of early information about the Antarctic seals, which are classed by Mr. Nicolai Hansen, his zoologist, and others rather more fully than I have given, as

> The Crab-eating or White seal (*Lobodon Carcino-phagus*)
> Weddell's seal or the False Sea Leopard (*Lep-tonychotes Weddelli*)
> The Sea Leopard (*Ogmorhinus leptonyx*)
> Ross's seal (*Ommatophoca Rossi*).

Unfortunately poor Hansen died at Cape Adare on October 14, 1899.

Dr. W. S. Bruce of the *Scotia* and Monsieur Racovitzi appear to have helped zoologists a great deal by studying the habits of the seals, putting forward reasons for their teeth and claws, explaining that sea leopards alone eat penguins, fish and even birds, whilst the other species feed mainly on crustacea and euphorsia (or whale food). Some idea of the weights of the Antarctic seals is given by the different Antarctic expedition leaders, who put the average full-grown seal's weight at half a ton when properly fed.

Penguins. As an animal lover and also a bird lover, I should put Pekingese and Penguins as the most interesting of all the animal kingdom to watch. After these I would rather watch lion cubs. However, as there are no lions nor Pekingese in the desolate Antarctic, we may as well pass on to the various types of penguin to be met with in the Antarctic and its adjacent waters.

Surgeon-Commander G. Murray Levick has written a fascinating little book called *Antarctic Penguins*. Before and since its publication, considerable attention has been given to the habits and the whereabouts and appearance of these extraordinary creatures by South Pole explorers.

Of all the different penguin species the Adélie Land Penguin is the most numerous and the most amusing to watch.

From the explorer's point of view or taste he is the most appetising; properly prepared and thoroughly well cleaned from all traces of blubber the Adélie penguin tastes quite like hare, and is much improved by red currant jelly !

In South Victoria Land, Adélie Land and Graham Land the great Adélie penguin rookeries are to be found, and there are others, plenty of them, outside the Antarctic Circle. This interesting blunt-billed Adélie, which weighs from ten to twelve pounds, and is as much as thirty inches in length, has a black head and back, white chest, belly and legs, whilst his flippers are black with scale-like feathers on the upper side and white underneath.

Most penguins are edible, but not all explorers are willing to eat them. Dr. Cook, the American member of de Gerlache's expedition, describes Adélie penguin as like " a piece of beef and odiferous cod fish and a canvas backed duck roasted in a pot with blood and cod liver oil for sauce ! "

During the two Antarctic relief expeditions in which I took part, we had in the little 147-foot whaler *Morning* opportunities of visiting Adélie penguin rookeries at Cape Adare, the Possession Islands, Franklin Island, Cape Crozier and Cape Royds. We also met the active little Adélies in the pack-ice and on narrow paths up the side of hills and peaks on most of the islands off the Victoria Land coast.

Dumont d'Urville's pictures show them on the side

of water-worn icebergs—here, there and everywhere. They followed both *Morning* and *Terra Nova* in the open sea, in water leads, and on the floes in the pack-ice, and their squawks are audible for miles. The noise of a million penguin squawks is a roar that can never be forgotten. The pungent odour of a penguin rookery is not at all pleasant, although the guano is magnificent fertilizer.

During nesting time Adélies attack people walking through the rookeries if they look like coming too close to the nests, and peck savagely at one's knees and calves. They take quite a lot of beating off, for the Adélie penguin knows no fear. We managed to get two to New Zealand in 1903, but they soon found their way down to the sea from Quamby, the Fendalton home of my father-in-law, about eight miles up the River Avon.

The other far south penguin is the Emperor (*Aptenodytes Fosteri*) a great big fellow weighing on an average about seventy-five pounds. His colouring differs from the black and white Adélie by the introduction of a good deal of yellow, varying from chrome to a deep gamboge flash on the head and neck at the sides, while the beak is crimson and purple coloured, and salmon pink at the sides merging into blue-black on the top. There is none of the speed and activity of the Adélie to be found in the Emperor, which may be likened to a cumbersome battleship compared with the destroyer-like Adélie.

The back of the Emperor penguin is more bluish-grey than black, and he is as much as forty-five inches in length.

Regarding the Adélies, their nesting habits excited great interest, and I believe that Levick's and Ponting's accounts would easily win any penguin-description competition.

There appear to be more males than females in the Adélie empires, and the rogue penguin who hovers about the rookeries gives the young married couples a lot of trouble. Parenthood is the first duty of these penguins, whose enemies are the skua gull, the rogue penguin, the weather and possibly the barren mother who has an unpleasant habit of adopting eggs and chicks from which she takes a good deal of displacing.

Adélie penguins, these virile funny little entities, have an amazing navigational instinct and locality sense. Captain Fairchild, of the New Zealand Government steamer *Hinemoa*, paid a great deal of attention to penguins and their navigational methods when I was " in the flapper stage " as an Antarctic explorer. Fairchild used to visit the Auckland Islands, Campbells, Macquaries and the Chatham Islands and often heard and saw the penguins migrating. They appear to form in extended line abreast and swiftly cruise in search of their objective rookery, island or colony, and give their necessary alter-course signals by squawking and repeating the squawk up and down the line.

Anyway, if the skua gull is King of the Antarctic, the Adélie penguin is the pet of the Great White South, and most, if not all of us, who have joined the brotherhood of the Antarctic look back with real affection to our Adélie days.

Reverting to the Emperor penguin. In Scott's first expedition it was found that Cape Crozier was the largest breeding place, and in September 1903 Lieutenant Royds' sledge party found about two thousand full-grown birds, and was fortunate enough to secure seventeen eggs. Petty Officer Cross succeeded in bringing two Emperor penguin eggs back to the *Discovery* in her ice-bound winter quarters and there, housed in Dr. Wilson's cabin, the chicks were kept alive for a considerable time. Scott wrote an amusing account of the baby Emperor penguins in captivity. Like all young penguins they had huge appetites. The specimens of young birds captured, skua gulls, petrels and penguins, can be divided into two classes—those who over-ate until they died and those who starved until they died !

36

In Scott's last expedition Dr. Wilson, accompanied by Lieutenant Bowers and Apsley Cherry-Garrard, our assistant zoologist, made their renowned winter journey to Cape Crozier, partly to study the embryology of the Emperor penguins, but were disappointed to find only about a hundred—few enough compared with the two thousand or so when Lieutenant Royds' sledge party visited Cape Crozier nine years earlier. Half a dozen eggs were collected, and Wilson picked up rounded pieces of ice at the rookery, which the stupid Emperors had been cherishing, fondly imagining that they were eggs.

Like the Adélies, the maternal instinct of the female Emperor penguin is very strong.

Wilson killed three birds and found them very thickly blubbered, and the oil obtained from them burned well.

Wilkes, the United States explorer, secured an Emperor penguin in Peacock Bay, latitude 65° 55' S., 151° 18' E., near Adélie Land outside the Antarctic Circle, and Ross found considerable numbers of them near Louis Philippe Land and Joinville Island in latitude 63° 36' S., 54° W.

It is interesting to note that in the stomachs of the Emperor penguins, besides crustaceans, beaks of cuttle-fish, schizopods, fish-bones and pebbles were found.

King penguins, which are the only other known members of the genus *Aptenodytes* (*A. patagonica*), have not, as far as I know, been found within the Antarctic Circle. We met plenty of them in late winter in the Falkland Islands, 1904, and Scott found them in the Kerguelen Islands.

There are, of course, other breeds of penguins: crested penguins, "Gorfoos" or "Rock-Hoppers", "Macaroni" penguins and the "Jackass" penguins, but these are not denizens of the desolate Antarctic, and are found there very, very seldom.

Ringed or bridled penguins (*pygoscelis antarctica*) have

been found in great numbers in the Falklands, and sub-Antarctic islands, South Georgia, South Orkneys and South Shetlands, Louis Philippe Land and even as far south as Andvord Bay, which is only about one hundred miles north of the Antarctic Circle. Once, we know, at Cape Royds, James Murray—Shackleton's biologist—found a single ringed penguin at the end of the Adélies' breeding season.

Chapter Five

ANTARCTIC BIRDS

WHEN in 1902, as a boyish sub-lieutenant, I first sailed south in the auxiliary barque *Morning*, I had a very hazy idea of the bird life of Antarctica. Fortunately our captain, William Colbeck, had spent a winter at Cape Adare with Sir George Newnes' Southern Cross Expedition, which was commanded by Mr. Carsten Borchgrevinck, an Anglo-Norwegian, and which included a very conscientious Norwegian naturalist, Nicolai Hansen, who handed his knowledge of Antarctic birds on to Colbeck and his fellow explorers. The officers of the *Morning*, for over two years, kept a zoological log in which was recorded, every four hours, a list of all birds in sight. Apart from the birds we saw on passage to the ice, we kept a full record of what was in sight in the pack-ice, and what birds visited us while at the edge of the frozen sea when we were carrying out our two relief voyages to bring food, stores and fuel to the *Discovery* fast in the ice in McMurdo Strait.

Having disposed of the penguins, much too briefly I fear, I will first write a little about their principal enemies—the skua gulls—whose great value to explorers is their tasty and nourishing flesh. Roast skua is almost as tasty as wild duck. McCormick's Antarctic skua is a fine-looking grey-brown coloured squarely-built gull; his colour varies somewhat from light to dark brown, and according to Captain Scott late in April the plumage was definitely darker than in summer. One skua evidently followed Amundsen nearly, if not quite, to the South Pole in 1911, and we found him in latitude 87° 20' S.—750 miles inland—on January 3, 1912. We also saw two near the foot of the Beardmore Glacier on our outward journey. And so with the exception of man and Amundsen's sledge dogs the arrogant skua holds the Farthest South record of any living creature.

In Scott's first southern journey skua gulls were seen once or twice, and also by Shackleton in his 1907 expedition, quite a long way south.

Wherever there is a penguin rookery there sure enough is the skua. He preys unmercifully on the Adélie penguin, snatching the eggs away in his beak, and almost " elbows " the penguin off her nest. Skuas eat the young penguin chicks, and, according to Ponting, they eat their own chicks and other skuas' chicks as well.

The skuas are full of fight and attack human beings immediately if their nests are approached. I remember having to defend myself stoutly with a geological hammer in 1903 when landed at Franklin Island, and Ponting nearly lost his eye when attacked whilst filming a baby skua on its nest in McMurdo Strait. The skuas don't like human beings, and attacked the landing party when first they came ashore from the *Southern Cross*. Their sharp curved claws and powerful wings make them dangerous opponents, for the adult skua is over four feet from wing tip to wing tip. Fortunately they don't appear to strike with their beaks, which are curved at the end, with a nasty sharp point. Ponting is an enthusiast about their appearance, as well he might be ; he says of them : " Their plumage is a symphony in browns, varying from a soft fawn-coloured breast to rich, dark brown wing and tail feathers, which are well graduated, with lighter edges ; and often there is a golden tinge about the neck of the male. On the pinions there is a broad streak of white, which gives the birds a remarkably handsome appearance when on the wing ; this white band is less marked on the upper side of the feathers." He also says : " The skua gull's virtues are its personal appearance and its love of cleanliness. It has a passion for fresh water, and whilst the snow lakes were open on Cape Evans scores would congregate in the largest of these to gambol and cleanse themselves in the waters for hours on end . . ."

The crying of the skua gull sounds quite like that of the ordinary herring gull, which can be almost musical at times. Commander Murray Levick, whose book *Antarctic Penguins* is such a gem for bird lovers and zoologists, commenting on the cruelty of these skuas, says that when the penguin chicks are hatched the skua gull preys upon them in a most cruel manner, and should a chick wander away from the protecting old bird, a skua is almost certain to pounce upon and kill it. This it does by pecking its eyes out, after which with powerful strokes of its beak it gets to work on its back and quickly devours the kidneys.

The dead bodies of hundreds of chicks are seen strewn about the rookery, and especially in the neighbourhood of the skuas' nests, as very often they carry them there. All these dead chicks are seen to have two holes picked through their backs, one on each side corresponding to the position of each kidney.

Then there is the giant petrel, almost greedier than the skua. This bird, which is nearly as big as an albatross, although not so graceful, is the scavenger of the Antarctic seas, and comes along like a vulture to every spot where carcases and refuse of seals and penguins or fish are to be found in the pack-ice or on the beaches.

According to Dr. McCormick, surgeon of the *Erebus*, when, after leaving Kerguelen, the boatswain fell overboard and could not be saved, the giant petrels swooped at him as he struggled to keep afloat, and it is doubtful if they did not actually strike him with their bills; while A. G. Guillemard states that a sailor, who was picked up, had his arms badly lacerated in defending his head from the attacks of an " albatross " which may well have been this giant petrel whose beak is a ghastly-looking weapon indeed.

This giant petrel, which rejoices in the scientific name of *ossifraga gigantea*, is as big as a large albatross. In colour it is normally dark chocolate brown. The younger birds exhibit more or less white in their plumage. The albino giant petrel is not at all uncommon, and is frequently found in the pack-ice. More albinos are found in high southern latitudes than farther north-ward, and I well remember finding a huge albino giant petrel in the pack-ice, and conning the little *Morning* through open water leads after a disgustingly full albino that ran along the floes vainly attempting to take off and " shifting ballast " at both ends in its attempts to get away. Eventually, having failed to become air-borne, he gave up and I managed to shoot him with size three shot. The early Antarctic sealers named this bird " the Nelly ". It is in fact the vulture of the sea.

And turning from the repulsive to the dainty, one can find in and around Antarctica brown-backed and silver-grey petrels, pure-white ice petrels, Wilson's petrels and stormy petrels, all of which or most of which fall within the " dainty series ".

Then there are whale-birds, which are small grey prions, and terns, which are found in large numbers near the South Polar regions, and even within the Antarctic Circle.

The Wilson stormy petrel, which rejoices in the latin name of *oceanites oceanicus*, is a little bigger than the " Mother Carey's chicken ", but it has unusually long legs. Dr. McCormick observed this stormy petrel hovering like a swallow or martin over the mastheads of the *Erebus* and *Terror* and obtained specimens in Ross's voyage, which were placed in the British Museum.

Most of us youngsters with Scott, or searching for him in the *Discovery* days, favoured the snow-white ice petrel (*pagodroma nivea*) " with satin-like plumage, jet-black eyes and bill, and graceful flight "; probably it is the favourite of every Antarctic expedition and certainly it has been seen by every one of these.

The Antarctic petrel, or brown-back, is another favourite, which has twelve tail feathers, and so is the silver-grey petrel which has fourteen tail feathers. I managed to collect a few of the two latter species for Cape Town Museum when visiting Bouvet Island in 1934, and from what I have written it will be realized that summer cruising in the Southern Seas is not without its colour and attractions. Unfortunately for those who are compelled to winter, whether in ship or on shore, all the bird life leaves and, as I have said elsewhere, only the seals and the Emperor penguins remain during the winter darkness. Everything else moves north.

Admiral Byrd, the most modern and, I should say, the most experienced of all South Polar explorers now living, takes, however, a different view from mine. He looks upon the desolate Antarctic as a pale, beautiful sleeping princess who lies " in her frozen slumber . . . her dreams iridescent ice haloes around the sun and moon, her horizons painted with pastel shades of pink, gold, green and blue ".

As far as the albatross family is concerned no true albatross has been captured within the Antarctic Circle, although the sooty albatross (*phœbetria*) is often seen at the edge of the pack-ice. In 1902 when we sighted our first iceberg in 62° S., the albatross following in the wake of the *Morning* turned northward and left us.

Chapter Six

FISH, WORMS AND WHAT-NOT

COLD-WATER fishes always strike me as being much better to eat than warm-water fishes. Sole, turbot, halibut and cod, and, of course, salmon and trout, have no equal in the tropic seas. But the Antarctic fish are not very much in evidence, and there are many more little fish than big fish about.

Once in Scott's first expedition a good big fish was taken—and this is the story : Skelton, the chief engineer, devised a harpoon with hinged barbs which proved a most effective weapon. With a line attached, it was kept in readiness at one of the fishing holes close to the ship, and the keen sportsman would go out and wait by the hour " harpoon in hand, ready for the first unfortunate seal which should come up to breathe. The long wait in the cold was rather a drawback, but when at last a black snout appeared on the surface and the murderous weapon was plunged downwards, there was great excitement, and shouts brought assistance to haul in the line. . . ." One day there was a loud commotion when the watcher, seeing a disturbance in the water, plunged the harpoon down. It obviously touched something solid, the watcher ran back to the ship and told his friends that he had hit a big fish. Soon the harpoon line was being hauled in despite the fact that a very lively " something " was at the other end. It turned out to be a large seal and the man who claimed to have harpooned a big fish was ridiculed no end. However, like most fishermen, he stuck to his story, that there had been a big fish, and later on Skelton, examining the brash ice in the hole, found the headless

44

body of a large fish for which the *Discovery's* men had been fishing in vain. It proved to be a 40-pounder, and it had obviously been attacked by the seal which had beheaded it. Afterwards the seal was found to be a female with young, evidently short of food and very thin with an empty stomach. The seal had apparently attacked the fish but being tired out had not succeeded in capturing the edible part. Anyway the *Discovery's* men had a fine meal of delicate-tasting white flesh.

We put down the absence of big edible fish to the seals and sea leopards which form " the inshore patrol ".

The *Discovery*, frozen in for a whole summer and two winters in McMurdo Strait, got more edible fish than we did in Scott's last expedition from our winter quarters at Cape Evans. The reason was largely because the *Discovery's* seamen had much more spare time, and that there were far more petty officers, seamen and stokers in *Discovery's* crew than there were in our main landing party, which contained only five seamen and stoker petty officers.

Atkinson, our helminthologist and parasitologist, kept Nelson, our marine biologist at Cape Evans, under close surveillance in the matter of the fish caught in the latter's traps. Most of the fish caught were a species of *notothenia*, or (as the sailors called them) whiting, and until Atkinson had had their gills and insides under his microscope they were kept in custody. After that they were handed to the cook to be fed to men and dogs.

The three marine biologists, Hodgson, Nelson and Lillie, and Dr. Koettlitz, a specialist in phyto-plankton (plant-life of the surface waters), in Scott's two Antarctic expeditions seemed to find the Royal Navy and Merchant Navy seamen very helpful, and when I commanded the *Terra Nova* there was never any lack of volunteers to help the marine biologists with their hauls or catches. I must say that our biologists took every advantage of trawling in the open water and dredging wherever and whenever possible. Once we had reached the continental shelf Nelson and Lillie got busy, and when in latitude 73° the latter discovered a shoal in only 158 fathoms—a great discovery for us—he immediately put over the Agassiz trawl, which he dragged along the bottom for half an hour and then hauled in to find the net full of big-mouthed fish, worms, spiders, and anemones, sea-cucumbers, polyzoa, prawns, little fish like sardines, one spikey fish like nothing on earth, star-fish, and octopus, limpets with jointed shells, sponges, ascidians, isopods, and all kinds of sea lice; enough to keep Lillie busy for weeks.

Working through pack-ice, which varies in nature and thickness, our propeller often overturned bits which were rotting and very much honeycombed underneath. These showed a rotting-melon colour, yellowish-red, and if placed under a microscope revealed masses of diatoms, or microscopic plants.

Dr. Koettlitz did a lot of work in the *Discovery* and Scott, writing about this, said that it was strange to have sailed the Seven Seas for years in ignorance that such things were !

Lieutenant Rennick and Paymaster-Lieutenant Francis Drake, who took a delight in pulling the legs of Nelson and Lillie, especially the latter, used to ask the most absurd questions, and misuse statements they found in text-books :

. . . If, therefore, the expedition is provided with an ample supply of alcohol, the formation of good series of individuals is in every case to be recommended.

This statement by G. A. Boulenger, F.R.S., in his article on Deep Sea Fishes, was twisted round until in the second dog watch Nelson or Rennick would often produce a gin-bottle and half a dozen glasses in the " cad's cabin " and start a " biological cag ". We learnt a lot from these cags, half-serious and half-comic.

The code words were "ample supply of alcohol". We certainly learnt the names of a number of large size and minute decapods, isopods and so forth, molluscs, crustacea, and echinoderms, and the meaning and use of the "impedimenta" of our biological friends, and, what is more, we learnt to admire Sir Arthur Shipley and to enjoy his writings. It was to Shipley we largely owed the selection of our biologists. He was a great friend of Dr. Wilson, and a man with a flair for " getting over " his subject. After spending an evening with him when he was Master of Christ's College, Cambridge, I told him that if I had my life over again I would make Marine Biology my profession.

Nelson and Lillie certainly won the " ample supply of alcohol " leg-pull—they first won the sailors over to be their willing helpers, and then the officers. One seaman, Browning, became a sort of unofficial biologist, and I remember listening to him discussing worms with three of the crew. As far as I can remember, he told them that to be helpful they must divide worms into classes—thread worms, poly-cheat worms, anelid worms and so on. It was all very interesting, and Pennell and I decided that whenever possible Browning's services should be made available to the biologists. We did not know that a propeller-headed tapeworm would be named after me. It was found, I believe, in the stomach of a penguin. However, I am in good company, for Captain Scott, the great leader himself, had a tapeworm named after him which had been discovered in the stomach of a fish.

At one of our Antarctic gatherings where seamen, scientists and officers dined happily together I told Nelson the story of the old lady who was persuaded to purchase a couple of yellow-painted sparrows, believing them to be canaries, from a London costermonger. The costermonger made, apparently, a great to-do in carefully choosing the pair. The old lady watched him with interest, and when finally the little birds had been placed in a far too small cage, she asked, " How can you tell which is the male bird and which is the female bird ? " " Why, that's dead easy," said the coster. " Yer just gets a plate of worms and puts it out before the birds, and then the male bird picks out and eats all the female worms, while the female bird picks out the male worms." " But how can you tell which are the male worms and which are the female worms ? " asked the old lady. " 'Ere 'ere 'ere, Ma'am," replied the coster, " steady on, I'm a bird fancier, not a worm fancier."

Dr. Bruce, leader of the Scottish National Antarctic Expedition had the *Scotia* fitted up extraordinarily well for marine biological work, and he and his staff made valuable additions to our biological knowledge of Antarctica. His people caught a cuttle-fish in Scotia Bay over six feet in length. This dreadful-looking brute had evidently been injured in conflict with a Weddell seal ! The proof that the Weddell enjoys eating cuttle-fish, and not only shrimps, is given by Bruce and others, who have found the beaks of cuttle-fish in seals' stomachs amongst the undigested contents.

Fish were often found frozen in the ice, apparently having been chased into brash ice by seals or by bigger fish.

It seems somewhat unappetising, but Lieutenant Victor Campbell's party, marooned in Terra Nova Bay, caught a seal and found thirty-six *notothenia* in its stomach, which fish, when fried in blubber, they ate and found excellent !

In Charcot's second Antarctic expedition he describes an Adélie penguin, jumping on to the ice, holding in its beak a very big fish. Boland, one of his sailors, seized it and wrested it from the penguin " who became furious —in a perfect frenzy of rage it accompanied the robber right back to the ship protesting ".

There is a good little summary of biological work carried out on board the *Terra Nova* in *Scott's Last*

Expedition, volume II, written by D. G. Lillie, and I love its opening lines, so typical of Scott's loyal scientific staff.

Lillie begins : " Captain Scott, with his characteristic thoroughness, made it possible for scientific work to be carried out by the ship's party, not only on their three summer visits to the Antarctic, but also during the two winters spent in New Zealand, and on the outward and homeward voyages."

I believe that both Lillie and Nelson are no longer with us. Nelson also contributed some remarks on marine biology, including the work undertaken from the Cape Evans shore station, during the two years Scott's expedition wintered there.

Chapter Seven

EARLY TWENTIETH-CENTURY VISITORS

WE are only half-way through the twentieth century, which has been described by Edith L. Elias, and by others as well, as the age of investigation.

Up in my mother-in-law's mountain home in Norway I chanced to open a book in which I found the inscription " *Til Richard fra Cato med tak for hyggelige dage i Hobart* 27–2–30 ".

The volume in question was the *Book of Polar Exploration* by Edith L. Elias, published by Harrap, with a foreword by my old expedition mate, R. E. Priestley, M.C., M.A., D.Sc., geologist to the Shackleton Expedition of 1907–9, and to Scott's last expedition—and now Vice-Chancellor and Principal of Birmingham University.

Edith Elias has the best psychological appreciation of the great Polar explorers of any writer of Arctic or Antarctic books. One sentence of hers I can never forget. She says of Mawson " . . . that no name is more respected among the men who have themselves been in Arctic Seas ".

Of the early twentieth-century visitors and their work I propose next to write. I shall take Scott, Shackleton, Mawson and Amundsen in that order, which to me seems the obvious one.

I am the last living man to speak to Scott—it was an unforgettable occasion—when on January 4th, 1912, nearly forty years ago, in latitude 87° 35' S., 145 geographical miles from the South Pole, the last supporting party (of which I was in charge) said good-bye.

Of my great leader I wrote in the book *South With*

Scott, first published by Collins in 1921 : " Certainly no living man could have taken Scott's place effectively as leader of our expedition—there was none other like him. He was the Heart, Brain and Master."

And now for a brief account of the work of Captain Robert Falcon Scott in the desolate Antarctic.

His first expedition left England in the summer of 1901 with a carefully selected company of officers, scientists and seamen—these mainly from the Royal Navy—in the specially built exploring ship *Discovery*.

The " Guardian Angel " of this expedition was Sir Clements Markham, President of the Royal Geographical Society, himself an old Arctic explorer, who as a junior naval officer had acted as geographer to the Abyssinian expedition.

With Scott was Shackleton, whose name, after Scott's, is perhaps the best known of the modern Antarctics. He had that lovable gentleman, artist, zoologist and doctor of medicine, Edward Adrian Wilson, with him, and Reginald Skelton, who was to become Engineer-in-Chief of the Navy ; Armitage, who had already served in the Arctic, as his second-in-command, and such naval men as Edgar Evans, who accompanied Scott to the Pole itself ; Wild, who became Shackleton's second-in-command, and Lashly and Crean, who made the 1,500-mile sledge journey of his last supporting party. Next to Armitage came Lieutenant Royds and then Lieutenant Michael Barne, who had been a sub-lieutenant in the flagship *Majestic* when Scott was her first lieutenant and fleet torpedo officer.

Scott very soon mastered the early history of Antarctic exploration—Weddell's and Biscoe's and Balleny's tracks were imprinted on his brain ; he always looked on Weddell's high latitude of 74° as a remarkable achievement, and when following in Ross's wake, more than half a century later, he added vastly to that explorer's magnetic, hydrographical and geographical surveys.

The *Discovery* sailed from New Zealand on Christmas Eve, 1901, when Scott said good-bye to civilization for more than two years and steered south to the gales, fogs, bergs and pack, which he negotiated skilfully in his strong little ship. Entering the Ross Sea, he sighted Victoria Land after obtaining a deep-sea sounding of 1,480 fathoms, which told him that he was on the verge of the Antarctic land plateau and heralded his first look at the Antarctic Continent, whose peaks he could clearly distinguish more than a hundred geographical miles away.

The *Discovery* entered Robertson Bay and Scott landed at Cape Adare, where he found the hut left by Borchgrevinck of Sir George Newnes' Southern Cross Expedition, which had wintered there in 1899, this being the first party to winter on the shores of the Antarctic.

Scott left a record here as he did on his southward way at Possession Islands, Coulman Island, Franklin Island and Cape Crozier—the easternmost point of Ross Island—prior to heading eastward along the Barrier cliff. Before doing this the *Discovery* crept slowly through inshore pack, and on January 21, less than a month out from New Zealand, she steamed right into McMurdo Sound, and proved it no longer a bay. Scott disproved the existence of the Parry Mountains, and from what he saw in McMurdo Sound was guided eventually to make his winter quarters in the south-west corner of Ross Island.

The expedition landed on the Great Ice Barrier, and Scott, brave sailor and fine leader, made a balloon ascent in the inlet he called Balloon Bay. His view from the balloon showed the *sastrugi* or snow-waves on the Barrier surface with which he became so familiar on his many sledging journeys.

But at the end of January something occurred of far greater moment than a balloon ascent; running into a deep bay and approaching the great slab of solid-looking pack-ice which lay ahead of him, he found long, undulating slopes, and swelling mounds, which turned out to be new land! This he named King Edward VII Land, after the reigning monarch.

Dr. Wilson made a beautiful water-colour, showing the purple sea in the foreground, backed by the Barrier cliffs, most truly and cleverly drawn, then the lone Barrier surface bounded by the hilltops in white and dark purple shades, beyond which are gold and copper-hued clouds surmounted by that sad, heavy cloudbank, which tells of approaching winter.

The altitude was calculated as between two thousand and three thousand feet, for the highest peaks and the snow-covered ridges and undulations appeared uniformly white, except for a few outcrops of rock, with occasional crevasses.

The ice-walls that beset this hitherto unvisited country rose to a height of 280 feet. They were all photographed by Skelton and sketched by Wilson, and so Scott's first Antarctic venture records have been enriched by good illustrations.

The *Discovery* winter quarters were established in 78° S., 167° E., in a small bay protected from the northward by a little spit of land called Hut Point, on which a magnetic observatory was erected; Scott spent two winters here. The main sledging expeditions were Scott's southern journey over the Barrier ice—in this, accompanied by Dr. Wilson and Shackleton, Scott reached latitude 82° 17′ S.; Lieutenant Royds made a journey south-eastwards over the Barrier, Lieutenant Barne south-westward to the entrance of the inlet which now bears his name; Armitage carried out pioneer journeys to the glaciers which connect with the inland plateau of Victoria Land; and Scott after the second winter made a remarkable journey up the Ferrar glacier and into the heart of that ice-capped plateau—right up on to the plateau summit, which he describes as " this terrible, limitless expanse of snow " and " so fearsomely monotonous ".

During this particular sledge journey, Scott, Evans and Lashly covered practically 1,100 miles at an average of 15½ miles a day, and climbed heights which totalled nearly 20,000 feet.

Unfortunately, when the relief expedition in the little whaler *Morning* came back with the news that the *Discovery* was held in the grip of the heavily frozen sea and compelled to face her second winter at Hut Point, the Government flew into a panic and despatched a second relief expedition, with two ships *Morning* and *Terra Nova* carrying 32 tons of gun-cotton and orders which amounted to " blast the *Discovery* out or else bring back her crew ".

It may be mentioned that thanks to Scott's record, placed as already described, we in the first relief expedition had followed his progress on what I call " a great Antarctic paper chase ". From a second record, left at Cape Crozier, we learnt the *Discovery's* whereabouts, and bringing back Shackleton, who was suffering from scurvy, and half a dozen others, Captain Colbeck (who commanded both relief expeditions) was able to give the Admiralty a comprehensive account of Scott's work, and whereabouts.

Colbeck pointed out that the first winter had been unusually severe and the ice conditions abnormal. However, the *Terra Nova* was purchased, and after the second relief voyage had contacted Scott, and the *Discovery* had been set free, the three ships sailed in company for New Zealand and home.

After taking part as a youngster in both relief expeditions, I was appointed second-in-command of Scott's next South Pole venture. Scott's second and last expedition history is well known to most Britons. As a young lieutenant I was put in charge of the Dundee whaler *Terra Nova*, and the expedition was fitted out to cover two Antarctic winters, although it was decided not to keep the ship south but to build huts instead. The main expedition wintered at Cape Evans, some fifteen miles north of the *Discovery's* old winter quarters, and from this point, after several depot-laying trips and other sledge journeys had been made and a great deal of scientific knowledge acquired—geological, hydrographical, zoological, geodetic and physical—and a special study of ice structure and glaciation made, the sledging season commenced. Winter journeys, notably that by Wilson, Lieutenant Bowers and Cherry-Garrard, added to our Antarctic knowledge : temperatures as low as 77° below zero were lived through with no other protection but sleeping-bags and light tents ; valuable spring and summer journeys were carried out by the physiographer and geologist and the great nine-hundred-mile journey to the Pole itself was made by Scott, Wilson, Captain Oates, Lieutenant Bowers, and Chief Petty Officer Evans. Dogs, ponies and motor sledges were used, the ponies dragging the food supplies to the foot of the Great Beardmore Glacier, which Shackleton had discovered and ascended in 1903. Scott was helped by a system of supporting parties which turned back in 81° 15′, 83°, 85° and 87½° S., and on January 4, 1912, the last supporting party, which had given up one of its number to make more easy the final dash and the long homeward trek, said good-bye to Scott and turned northward. I had charge of this hazardous return. With me were Chief Stoker Lashly and Petty Officer Crean. It was a disappointment to my party that we could not all go to the Pole—a great disappointment, but we had been brought up to treat misfortunes with a smile and successes with a cheer.

We took enough food to get us back to latitude 87° where we had established a depot. We made a short march with Scott's team to see that, with their load increased by what we had brought along, they could manage without unduly straining. They got along finely for three or four miles, then they halted and said good-bye. We shook hands all round, and we felt very moved as we looked into their eyes, and at their smoke-begrimed, bearded faces.

There were cakes of ice on their beards, weather-scars, split lips, and frost-bite marks, but their rugged faces had become very dear to us, and it seems a few weeks rather than nearly forty years since that memorable " good-bye ".

The return of the last supporting party, which nearly ended in disaster, is a story which has been fully published in *South With Scott*, but as Helmer Hanssen in his *Voyages of a Modern Viking* says, " The distance we went, as the crow flies, was more than 2,500 kilometres " (Lashly and I dragged our sledge for precisely the same distance without any help from dogs or ponies whatever). Hanssen continues :

> . . . but Scott had even farther to go. We started with 52 dogs and came back with 11, and many of these wore themselves out on the journey. What shall we say of Scott and his comrades, who were their own dogs ? Anyone with any experience would take off his hat to Scott's achievement. I do not believe men ever have shown such endurance at any time, nor do I believe there ever will be men to equal it. All I can say is : Honour be to him and his men.

In this year 1949 when the film *Scott of the Antarctic* is being shown throughout the English-speaking world, it seems almost superfluous for me to write even an abbreviated story of the Great Sledge Journey. The full story is best told by Scott himself in *Scott's Last Expedition*. It has been told and re-told by those who have taken part and those who have not even been in the Southern Hemisphere, much less within the Antarctic Circle. Stephen Gwynn in his book, one of the Golden Hind series, pays tremendous tribute to my great leader, who, with his four companions—Dr. Wilson, Captain

Shackleton, Scott and Wilson before
their first long southern journey.

On the next two pages :
Looking west from Barne Glacier to Cape Barne.

The author and Edward Nelson excavating
an ice-cave for the storage of meat.

L. E. G. Oates, Lieutenant H. R. Bowers and Chief Petty Officer Edgar Evans—gave his life for "the quest of knowledge in the uttermost parts of the Earth", as Dr. Simpson, his comrade of the desolate Antarctic, has so aptly described it.

Sir Douglas Mawson describes Scott's South Polar journey as a marvel of human strength and endurance.

Admiral Sir Reginald Skelton, Scott's comrade in the Service and comrade in his first Antarctic journey, has written in a private letter : " Anything that anybody could write to explain Scott's greatness would be poor stuff, after what he has written himself on his last journey —and I am not sure I like the word ' greatness '—he was better than that. Otherwise you would not have had Wilson following him a second time." This, to my mind, is the best tribute of all.

And so may I set down just this—the last we saw of Scott and his companions was a tiny black speck on a great white horizon of ice. From the time we left them an evil spirit seemed to dog Scott's footsteps. Whenever and wherever he needed good luck he met with misfortune and even disaster, whereas exactly the opposite can be said of the short-handed last supporting party, who seemed to have, truly, a guardian angel watching over them.

Soon after we separated we were overtaken by a blizzard but, the wind blowing strongly from the south, we were able to make use of it by setting the floor cloth of our tent as a sail, and we drove northwards at a fine speed, making unbelievable progress. The dust-fine particles of driving snow stung our eyes and almost blinded us and we got to the eastward of our intended route ; so much so that in the end we took what, to my mind, was the greatest hazard of my life and tobogganed over the Shackleton Ice Falls, which from start to finish descended over two thousand feet. It meant facing tremendous drops. The travelling surface was windswept and consequently too easy, for the sledge would charge down a slippery slope of blue ice and capsize time after time. I shall never forget that exciting descent, the speed of the sledge at one point must have been sixty miles an hour. The three of us were lying face downwards on the sledge when suddenly it seemed to spring into the air—we had left the ice and shot over one yawning crevasse before we had known of its existence almost. I do not imagine we were more than a second in the air, but in that brief space of time I looked at Crean, who raised his eyebrows as if to say " What next ? " ; then we crashed on to the ice ridge beyond this crevasse, the sledge capsized and rolled over and over, dragging us with it until it came to a standstill.

How we ever escaped uninjured is beyond me to explain, and what is more our guardian angel, or Providence if you like, was still with us when we landed, for we found ourselves quite close to the Upper Glacier depot where the third supporting party, under our gallant little naval surgeon, Atkinson, had turned northward and said good-bye.

This three days of blizzard weather meant severe setbacks for Scott. The hard southerly wind decreased the speed of the sledge party, a dead head wind which caused frostbite on feet, fingers and faces, and when at last the weather cleared, Bowers' sharp eyes detected a black speck on the horizon which turned out to be a flag flying from a sledge runner buried in the snow. When Scott and his men came up to it they found dog tracks, ski tracks and sledge tracks which told them that the valiant Norseman, Roald Amundsen, was before them.

Scott and his four loyal companions reached the South Pole on January 17, 1912, to find a little brown tent with the Norwegian flag fluttering from a white staff. Below the flag was a broad pennant, white with the word " *Fram* " in dark blue. Inside the tent Scott found a note from Amundsen and also a record giving the names of the five Norwegians :

> Roald Amundsen
> Olav Olavson Bjaaland
> Helmer Hanssen
> Sverre H. Hassel
> Oscar Wisting

telling that they reached the South Pole on December 16, 1911.

On November 29, 1948, the tragedy of Scott's long nine hundred mile northward march was unfolded in the film *Scott of the Antarctic* which I sadly watched with a great company including Her Majesty the Queen, the Duke of Edinburgh and Princess Margaret. The company also included one or two who had marched South with Scott, and several others who had served in one or both of his Antarctic expeditions. Two of Scott's sisters were there, Wilson's brother and sister, Miss Violet Oates, and Frederick Ranalow (Oates' elder sister's husband), Bowers' two sisters, Chief Petty Officer Evans' widow and Mrs. Atkinson, widow of Surgeon-Commander Atkinson, D.S.O., A.M. John Mills, who played the part of Scott so ably, and Harold Warrender, who took the part of Edward Adrian Wilson, and, in fact, all those who supported them, did a great service to the youth of Britain and to us older ones too, for they brought to life the story which proved that Peace hath her Victories no less renowned than War.

The film emphasized those setbacks and reverses which followed and dogged Scott's footsteps over that great white way. The failure of Evans, the strongest man in the party, due to a badly cut finger, followed by frost-bite and a tragically unfortunate fall, and then an even worse fall which must have injured his brain ; and then a further tragedy which caused Captain L. E. G. Oates to drop astern of the team and fail, mainly due to his having tended poor Edgar Evans, bandaging his frost-bitten hands and feet, a sacrifice that no doubt caused the "Soldier", as we called him, to suffer severe frost-bites which directly incapacitated him. Evans died at the foot of the Beardmore Glacier and was buried near Desolation Camp, where the last of our ponies had been shot—five of the poor little beasts.

Oates deliberately gave up his life on March 17, 1912, his thirty-second birthday, when, realizing that the salvation of Scott, Wilson and Bowers depended on his self-sacrifice, he walked out of the tent in the driving snow, staggering out into that pitiless waste until he could go no farther, when he fell and died in his tracks.

Scott wrote : " We knew that poor Oates was walking to his death, but, though we tried to dissuade him, we knew it was the act of a brave man and an English gentleman. We all hope to meet the end in a similar spirit, and assuredly the end is not far."

Scott, Wilson and Bowers struggled on for another three marches and on the night of Monday, March 19, they got to within eleven miles of One Ton Depot, where there was food for the whole sledge party, which should have made their return to our winter quarters a reasonably straightforward business, but, alas, it was not to be.

Scott had confidently looked forward to higher temperatures, fair winds and better surfaces, instead of which he got temperatures well below zero, −40° at noon even, and either head winds or calms, and mostly blizzard weather and surfaces like sand, positively with no glide in them.

From March 20–29, 1912, it was one long blizzard, and with the wind howling all about them their chances of reaching One Ton Camp dwindled and faded altogether. They had food for two days and fuel for one hot meal, and then for a whole week in cold that beat

Russian winter, Scott, Wilson and Bowers nobly awaited the end.

Scott's message to the public is a saga in English literature. These were the real men, proud of their country, proud of their profession, men whose memories alone are an inspiration. What an example to the youth of our nation in whose hands is the key to power—the key to our future and our freedom. What a splendid example this grand man Scott gave us all when almost at his last gasp, after the longest sledge journey on record, he wrote, with the pencil dropping from his frozen fingers: "How much better has this all been than lounging in too great comfort at home."

Shackleton. Shortly after I took over the command of H.M.S. *Carlisle* on the China station in 1921, my commander-in-chief, Admiral Sir Alexander Duff, talking about Antarctic exploration, suddenly asked me: "What sort of fellow really is Shackleton?" I answered: "Well, sir, if you call Scott the Jellicoe of Antarctic exploration, and Shackleton the Beatty, you've got their psychology in a nut-shell! Both were born leaders, one a great, brave, scientific sailor, the other fearless, imaginative and gallant like a born cavalry leader."

No man I ever met had a greater flair for getting out of tight corners than Shackleton.

Both Scott and Shackleton have enriched English literature by their writings. Volume I of *Scott's Last Expedition* can be picked up again and again—it describes the Antarctic perfectly—no exaggeration, no superfluity of words, no failure to appreciate the work of other explorers.

And in Shackleton's case, he possessed better than any man I have known the gift of choosing the right words from his own rich vocabulary and his vast fund of quotations—this sailor-explorer and true poet of the sea.

The crash of the bows in the ice-pack ;
The sob of the tilted floe ;
The creak of the weighted sledges ;
The whine of the dogs as we go.

is a type-specimen of Shackleton's verse.

It was Shackleton's personality that made Scott
select him with Dr. Wilson to be one of the three who
were to make the first long sledge journey southwards ;
that pioneer journey that started off on November 2,
1902, under Scott's own leadership.

The full story, a very fine story, is to be found in
volume II of Scott's first book, *The Voyage of the Discovery*.

The little team, aided by a supporting party of twelve
men under Lieutenant Michael Barne (who left three
days earlier), left *Discovery's* winter quarters with five
sledges and nineteen dogs and reached latitude 82° 17' S.

Michael Barne's supporting party continued, marching
independently, until November 15, and then, helping to
readjust the sledge loads, made all ready for Scott's
final effort, and returned to the winter quarters.

" November 25. Before starting to-day I took a
meridian altitude, and to my delight found the latitude
to be 80° 1'. All our charts of the Antarctic regions show
a plain white circle beyond the eightieth parallel ; the
most imaginative cartographer has not dared to cross
this limit and even the meridional lines end at the circle.
It has always been our ambition to get inside that white
space, and now we are there the space can no longer be a
blank ; this compensates for a lot of trouble." I quote
this from the leader's diary because it marks a tremendous
forward stride in the history of Antarctic exploration.

On this far south journey Scott, Shackleton and Wilson
discovered two great mountains, which they named
Mount Markham and Mount Longstaff, after Sir Clements
Markham and Lieut-Colonel Longstaff, the two great
supporters of the expedition.

Things have moved rapidly since that time. The return from 82° 17' had one or two unfortunate episodes, as for example on December 3 when the pemmican bag for the week was slung alongside a tin of paraffin and became strongly impregnated with the oil, and that day in lighting the primus Scott burnt a hole in the tent. He writes : " I did not heat the pot sufficiently before I began to pump and a long yellow flame shot up and set light to the canvas. I do not think I should have noticed what had happened at first, but luckily the others were just approaching, and rushed forward to prevent further damage. As it was there was a large hole, which poor Shackleton had to make shift to repair during our last lap ; it is not much fun working with a needle in the open at the midnight hours, even though the season happens to be summer."

A couple of days later, the little party found that there had been some wastage of paraffin from the capsizing of the sledge—this taught an important lesson that far, far greater care must be taken of this vital commodity.

Then came some disappointing, poor marches, and then the glass of one of the chronometer watches, on which accurate observations for longitude depended, was broken—Scott writes that future expeditions should be supplied with a larger number of chronometer watches than his sledge party carried.

On December 6 a dire calamity—the dog " Spud " was absent from his sleeping place on the trace. Captain Scott found him lying on the sledge with his head on the open mouth of the seal meat bag ! He writes " One glance at his balloon-like appearance was sufficient to show what had happened. As one contemplated the impossibility of repairing the mischief and of making him restore his ill-gotten provender, it was impossible not to laugh ; but the matter is really serious enough ; he has made away with quite a week's allowance of our precious seal meat. How he could have swallowed it all is the wonder, yet, though somewhat sedate and somnolent, he appears to suffer no particular discomfort from the enormously increased size of his waist. We found, of course, that he had gnawed through his trace, but the seal meat bag will be very carefully closed in future."

By December 8, Scott's dog-team was going steadily down hill. Half the dogs scarcely pulled at all, and all were weakening rapidly and making the poorest of marches, and on December 10 the party only covered two miles. The dog " Snatcher " died that day and was eaten by his "comrades", who found his flesh more to their liking than their dried fish diet.

Then came bad snow surfaces and a high air temperature, +27°, which made the three men hot and stuffy.

Despite the various setbacks all three learnt from their sledging experience. We who followed in after expeditions made use of this experience and thereby gained great advantage.

Unfortunately, the strain of this first southern journey caused the loss of the dog team, and indeed scurvy, that dread disease and enemy of the Polar explorer, made its appearance, Shackleton suffering most. Wilson, who never missed an opportunity of making beautiful and useful sketches, was badly afflicted with snow-blindness, which he described as " an almost intolerable stabbing and burning of the eyeballs ".

When at last, burnt quite black from the sun, with their hair uncomfortably long and in matted locks, their faces lined and wrinkled and looking most worn and haggard, the Southern Three won through, they were a trio of exhausted down-and-out tramps, very different from the broad-shouldered stalwarts who had left the *Discovery's* winter quarters three months before.

We in the *Morning* moored to the edge of the frozen sea were apprised of Scott's home-coming by a Union Jack hoisted on Hut Point, nearly eight miles away.

For a whole month we awaited the break-up of the
sea ice, which was expected, but there was little indication of this, and when, at the end of February, five miles
of frozen sea intervened between Hut Point and the
little *Morning* plans were completed for her departure,
and eight of the *Discovery's* crew were sledged over to
the relief ship for passage back to New Zealand. Poor
Shackleton's health was now too bad for him to face
another winter, and on March 2, 1904, he sledged over to
the *Morning* with most of the *Discovery's* crew to spend
their last night in our company on board. We had a
sing-song and merry-making which lasted far into the
night, during which the temperature fell to below zero
and young ice covered the surface of the sea in McMurdo
Sound. Next morning, after breakfast, we had some
difficulty in getting our little *Morning* free—she had been
frozen in with ice several inches thick during that last
night. However, by running both ships' companies
from side to side we worked up a good old deep-sea roll
and managed to get our ship free. Then Scott, his
officers and men scrambled over the side, our crew ran
aloft and loosed all sail, when, the last good-byes having
been said and cheers exchanged, we turned our little
ship's head northward, set topsails and top gallant sails
and headed once more for civilization, in the shape of
our beloved New Zealand.

Poor Shackleton nearly broke his heart at being
invalided. He often used to spend part of the night
watches with Doorly and myself and we learnt to know
him well.

Shackleton was a man hungry and thirsty for great
hazards, yet full of laughter and cheerfulness; a strong
believer in the value of Polar exploration, which he
thought made for enterprise, audacity, forward-looking,
hard-living and moral steadfastness.

Harold Begbie, the author and distinguished journa-
list, gave me his book *Shackleton—a Memory* the year

that his hero died. Facing the title page is a very brief quotation from William Blake :

> Great things are done when men and mountains meet ;
> This is not done by jostling in the street.

In 1907 Shackleton, having planned and organized the British Antarctic expedition, picked from a long list of volunteers a first-class company which included Captain Rupert England, formerly chief officer of the Antarctic relief ship *Morning*, and John King Davis, as his chief officer (and later captain), Professor Edgeworth David, F.R.S., as chief of his scientific staff, Dr. Douglas Mawson, physicist, Raymond Priestley, geologist, and several of those who had served in the National Antarctic Expedition or National Antarctic Relief Expeditions, including that remarkable little Elizabethan sailor, Frank Wild, and another prominent *Discovery* petty officer, Joyce, and last, but by no means least, the most famous of all Antarctic boatswains, Alf Cheetham, a wiry little Yorkshireman who came with Captain Colbeck from the *Montebello* to the *Morning* in 1902. (He and I were actually the first to join the ship and I became very much attached to him. After serving as Shackleton's bo'sun in the *Nimrod* he served as bo'sun and ice-master in the *Terra Nova* on Scott's last expedition, and then again with Shackleton, and I believe with Mawson as well. He lost his life the day before Armistice Day, 1918, when his ship was torpedoed by an enemy submarine.)

Purchasing the stoutly-built little wooden *Nimrod*, Shackleton had her altered and fitted out by the firm of R. & H. Green, of Blackwall, who had had a good deal of experience in handling wooden exploring ships, and then on July 30, 1907, the expedition left London for Lyttelton, N.Z., and the South Polar regions.

Shackleton's three main objectives were :

To reach the South Pole.

To plant the Union Jack at the South Magnetic Pole.

To investigate the Great Ice Barrier,

but, apart from the foregoing, Shackleton had an ambitious and comprehensive scientific programme which was placed under the directorship of Professor T. W. Edgeworth David.

Before leaving Lyttelton ten Manchurian ponies, nine dogs and a 12–15 h.p. Arrol-Johnston motor car and as much coal as the bunkers and deck space could hold were embarked.

Shackleton's Irish imagination caused him to charter the collier *Koonya* to tow him down to the pack-ice, thereby extending his steaming radius.

The *Nimrod* sailed from N.Z. on New Year's Day, 1908, and after a very rough passage through the mountainous seas and the " Roaring Forties ", where the wind reached hurricane force, the *Nimrod's* bulwarks were smashed in and two of the ponies so injured that they had to be shot, the *Nimrod* and the *Koonya* parted company when fairly surrounded by icebergs.

Shackleton, with splendid steaming radius available, proceeded eastward along the Great Ice Barrier to the position of Balloon Bay, which had disappeared. In its stead was a wide opening, which he christened the Bay of Whales. It was here in January 1911 that the *Fram* with Amundsen's expedition was sighted by the *Terra Nova* in Scott's last expedition, whilst a landing was being sought for Lieutenant Campbell, and a small party of Scott's men. Shackleton tried to extend Scott's discoveries in the vicinity of King Edward VII Land, but was compelled to turn westward after encountering very heavy ice, which caused the *Nimrod* to leak.

Much against his will, he was forced to choose Cape Royds for his winter quarters, being more than twenty miles north of where the *Discovery* had been frozen in. His shore party consisted of fifteen scientists and sailors and included Professor David, Dr. Mawson and R. E.

Priestley, who subsequently served as a geologist with Scott.

Shackleton built a medium-sized hut where he wintered in 1908, and whilst David, Mawson and Dr. MacKay made a journey to the north-westward and reached the Magnetic Pole, Shackleton with Lieutenant Adams, his second-in-command, Dr. Eric Marshall, his surgeon and cartographer, and Frank Wild made what will always stand out as one of the greatest sledge journeys in history. Four ponies, each dragging a sledge of over six hundred pounds, commenced what has been described as " One of the greatest hunger marches ". His party built beacons, cairns of ice to guide them homeward, an example which Scott's men followed two years later. On November 26, 1908, Shackleton trod farther south than ever man had before. Passing Scott's first " farthest south ", 82° 17', every new mountain, every new feature of that extensive, high, glaciated land became Shackleton's own discovery.

The two great mountains Markham and Longstaff which Scott had placed on the map were succeeded by other grand peaks, and as Shackleton and his companions trod over virgin barrier ice, they grew amazed at their own southward progress.

On December 2 a great glacier showed up, which led almost due south through the mountains, and when Shackleton camped to have his lunch that day he made a momentous decision which he communicated to the other three, and that was that they should ascend this glacier which he subsequently named the " Beardmore ". Hopes ran high, so high that a small, reddish granite mountain was christened Mount Hope, and from its flat summit the southern group was further reconnoitred. Half-way up the glacier a massive, round-topped mountain was seen. Shackleton afterwards christened it the " Cloud Maker " as its summit was nearly always obscured by low stratus clouds. Unlike Scott, Shackleton managed to get a pony named "Socks" well on to the glacier itself. This proved to be a mistake, for poor "Socks" early on disappeared down a yawning chasm, the snow-bridge of which bore the weight of a man, but not that of a heavy pony. This loss meant a great deal to the men, who had counted on the pony meat to help feed them, as they won farther south. The passage up the glacier was a difficult one, but most interesting—fringed as it was by mountains, cliffs, and small glaciers. Fossils were found, and even coal, and a good rough sketch survey made ; a new mountain range, named after Queen Alexandra, was discovered on the western side of the Beardmore ; other ranges followed, named the Commonwealth and Dominion Ranges, in honour of their Australian expedition mates. Finally the Inland Plateau which Shackleton describes as "the bleakest and most horrible part of the earth" was gained, and in spite of crevasses and a compulsory reduction in their food allowance, with pretty low temperatures and often bad surfaces, the inimitable, witty, and lovable leader fought on to latitude 87°.

A further food reduction left the party weak, and the high altitude, more than 10,000 feet up as they were, gave them headaches and great lassitude.

But although his party were rapidly weakening, they managed to pull their sledge loads on until it became necessary, due to blizzards and other circumstances, to build a depot and push on, dragging not much more than seventy pounds per man. Shackleton and his comrades loyally took the risk of leaving that depot of food-stuffs out of sight of landmarks or any leading marks by which it could be located. Then came blizzard weather, and a gale, followed by frostbite and snow-blindness, and painful cuts on their faces.

On January 9, 1909, Shackleton realized that to go on farther meant death for them all, and then, in latitude 88° 23' S., a little flag presented to him by Queen

Alexandra was flown at his farthest south, and the Polar plateau taken possession of in the name of King Edward VII. They were only ninety-seven geographical miles from the South Pole, when they turned and commenced that terrible homeward march.

Fortunately, their old track showed up, and where their fur-clad feet had pressed down into the snow the force of the blizzard had swept the snow away all round, and little nine-inch-long shapes appeared, standing cheerfully above the surface like so many blancmange moulds —a chain of these frequently appeared to guide them on their way. This meant a very great deal; it spared unnecessary observations to be taken by theodolite and worked out with ice-bitten fingers in the meagre shelter of their now sadly worn tent.

The homeward march was a race with death, and, in spite of their small sledging ration, they marched as much as 26 miles in a day, and sometimes ran out of all their provisions, except cocoa and tea, on which they lived until they found their way on to the next depot. January 28 brought them back to the Barrier, and then even their rejoicing ceased, for Wild developed dysentery. This is indeed a bad business; it results often in hæmorrhage from the bowels, and the white snow is covered by patches of blood which are alarming to behold. The others were also attacked by dysentery. The red-letter day in Shackleton's diary came when they reached a well-marked depot laid down by a supporting party, but, in spite of this, Marshall nearly died, and it was only due to Shackleton's swift and successful decision and his unconquerable optimism that the party reached the old hut left by Scott in *Discovery* days. Shackleton's landing party was picked up by the *Nimrod*, which sailed for New Zealand on March 4, 1909, and brought back this heroic band to safety.

While the limelight was, as it were, focussed on Shackleton's southern journey, just as on Scott in the film which will help to perpetuate his memory, Professor David with Mawson and Alistair MacKay made a wonderful sledge journey to the Magnetic Pole.

Some assistance, to begin with, was given by the motor car, which dragged two sledge-loads totalling 856 lb. To quote from Professor David's narrative : "As soon as Day put the car on her second gear we sped over the floe ice at a rate of 14 miles an hour, much to the admiration of the seals and penguins." (Day was our motor engineer in Scott's last expedition. His nickname was Handy Andy.)

During the early part of the journey, after the car was dispensed with, when David camped for the night near a seal-hole the slumbers of the party were disturbed by the snorting and whistling of the seals as they came up for their blows, but these were nothing to the Emperor penguins, which awakened them by their chatter. I have never experienced this, although I have done hundreds of miles sledging on various duties over the frozen sea. Professor David, writing about this on October 10, said : " Evidently the Emperors had marched down on our tent during the night to investigate us, and the sounds they made may be described as something between the cackle of a goose and the chortle of a kookaburra. I saw four of them standing by the sledges and when they caught sight of me they were much interested, and the conversation between them became very lively. I have no doubt that they took us for penguins of an inferior type, and the tent for our nest. At any rate they were kind enough to take careful note of our doings and to give us a good send-off when we left them ! "

When David's party climbed on to the mainland on October 17 they hoisted the Union Jack and took possession of Victoria Land for the British Empire. God bless them.

When one remembers that Professor David was fifty-two when he made this outstandingly difficult journey, that he fell down crevasses, and took all this in his stride, one feels more than proud to number such men as Shackleton, David and Mawson among one's friends. Edith Elias, better than anyone, has turned the searchlight on to the Magnetic Pole party, and I quote her paragraph, which runs :

Three men, alone in a desert of snow, irritated to desperation by driving snow and suffering agonies from frost-bite, dragging an enormous load over all types of surface, the monotony of their toil broken only too often by narrow escapes at crevasses, their breath coming in jerks because of the rarity of the air, enduring all this willingly and even exultantly for the sake of accomplishing a task—this surely is a picture to stir the imagination of the most sluggish ! To do all this and then to come home quietly and modestly, boasting nothing of their achievement, here surely is greatness !

I cannot do better than continue in Edith Elias' language :

. . . January 1909 found them still pressing on, and on the 16th they arrived at their objective, the exact spot being calculated as latitude 72° 25' S., longitude 155° 16' E. The Union Jack was planted and Professor David declared aloud : " I hereby take possession of this area now containing the magnetic Pole for the British Empire." The three men then gave three cheers for the King, after which they thankfully turned their faces home. " We were," confesses Professor David, " too utterly weary to be capable of any great amount of exultation "—a sentence of most eloquent brevity.

Shackleton's next efforts were made in the re-named Norwegian whaler, which now became the *Endurance*. On this occasion he planned what was known as the " Trans-Antarctic Expedition," and secured the Whaler *Aurora* to sail from the New Zealand side whilst he himself intended to start with dog teams from the Wed-

72

dell sea. It was planned that the Ross Sea party should take stores for his use to the Beardmore Glacier and meet him at Mount Buckley where he first found coal. Shackleton had 70 dogs, and his plan for the Trans-Continental sledge journey was as bold as any ever made.

On December 5, 1914, Shackleton left South Georgia in the *Endurance*, entered the pack in 60° S., and penetrated a couple of degrees or so into it. By Christmas Day he had made some three hundred and fifty miles southing, but such gigantic floes were met with that further progress was held up until the ice loosened, and he advanced a further two hundred and fifty miles. He then came to open water in 69° 47' and, steaming and sailing through dark-green water, sighted an ice barrier and land, which was undoubtedly that discovered by the Scottish explorer, Dr. W. S. Bruce, in 1904. Shackleton passed Bruce's farthest south on January 12, 1915. New land was named the "Caird Coast", and about this time the biologists made a great haul of specimens. After confirming other explorers', notably Filchner's, discoveries, and shortly after a near approach was made to Vahsel Bay, Shackleton's expectations of landing on January 19 were frustrated by close pack besetting the ship. Failing to work free they prepared to winter in the ice. Nothing daunted, Shackleton put his dogs out on the floe and trained them, and his men as well, keeping up their spirits in the Shackletonian way, and preparing a provision stack lest the *Endurance* should be crushed.

Winter was soon upon them, and, although the ship was once or twice nearly crushed, she withstood the pressure until long after mid-winter's day, when more screwing and grinding caused the *Endurance* to lift and list and finally fall back into the water. By mid-October the ice pressure had increased seriously, until the *Endurance* listed nearly 30°.

The end was not far off now, and late on October 26 the ship began to leak badly, and was finally crushed and annihilated. Shackleton preserved some extraordinary pictures of the last of the *Endurance*.

His foresight in making "ocean camp" on a very thick floe saved his crew. The floe was drifting north, and the period of waiting was anxious. The ice was gradually breaking up and when March arrived a swell was noticed. On the 23rd Shackleton sighted Joinville Island, and on April 8, 1916, he saw Elephant Island, and realized that he must make this land as best he might, so on Sunday, April 9, embarking the expedition in three boats, he started for what he hoped would be safety.

His men behaved magnificently, singing as they worked at the oars among heaving and grinding floes. After many adventures and escapes that fell nothing short of a miracle, a landing was made on Elephant Island by all three boats without losing a single man.

The story of the party's hardships and sufferings is a terrible one. And the voyage of the whale boat *James Caird* with Worsley, Crean, McCarthy, Vincent and McNeish, with Shackleton in command, is the story of the finest boat journey on record. The men's sleeping-bags were soaked in icy salt water, and on watch three at a time, one steering and the other two baling, they lived through a legend. The ice-beset boat nearly sank with the weight of the frozen sea water which encased it, and on May 6 the boat nearly met her end. A gigantic wave broke through the white-capped seas, the men found themselves in "a heaving chaos of tortured water ; but somehow the boat lived through it. . . . We baled with the energy of men fighting for life . . . and after ten minutes of uncertainty, we felt the boat renew her life beneath us. . . ." And so the story goes on until they mercifully reach South Georgia.

How this grand man Shackleton made contact with those modern Vikings, the whaling crews there, would take a great deal of space, but in the whaler *Southern Sky* he made his first attempt to relieve the Elephant Island party, failed, then tried again in the Uruguayan steamer *Instituto de Pesca* and this time also failed, then a third attempt in the little schooner *Emma* which likewise failed, and finally a fourth and successful attempt was made in the Chilean Government steamer *Yelcho*. When the 22 men, so finely commanded by Frank Wild, were found all well after four and a half months' separation, the first words they uttered were not of joy at their rescue, but : " Thank God the boss is safe."

Having seen to the safety of the *Endurance* company in the Weddell Sea, Shackleton's immediate anxiety was to make sure of the safe return of the *Aurora's* crew, which had also suffered disaster, for the ship had broken from her moorings in McMurdo Sound and drifted northward while making her way back to New Zealand. However, she was repaired and overhauled. The ship again visited McMurdo Sound, embarked those left behind and on February 9, 1917, arrived back in New Zealand. The Trans-Antarctic journey was never made, but in spite of all that they went through only three men were lost in the entire expedition.

Shackleton's last Antarctic enterprise was made in the *Quest*. I saw this ship in Iceland and sadly shook my head. She was no ship for the South Polar ice. In her Shackleton had sailed in 1920. Short of funds, he had been unable to obtain a stout enough ship for the voyage. This little sealer of only 125 tons was too lively for heavy seas, and too slow to achieve much. Her engines gave trouble, the hull seemed wrong, and to me she looked like a floating coffin. She leaked badly but nevertheless managed to reach South Georgia and anchor at Grytviken on January 4, 1922, in the same place as the ill-fated *Endurance* had done. Before he turned in on the night of January 4, 1922, Shackleton wrote in his diary :

At last, we came to anchor in Grytviken. A wonderful evening.

In the darkening twilight I saw a lone star hover
Gem-like above the bay.

And that was his last. He died that night, and when talking to the youth of our nation, I always quote those words he was so fond of :

Never for me the lowered banner,
Never the endeavour lost . . .

Chapter Eight

MAWSON'S MAGNIFICENT ACHIEVEMENTS

PROFESSOR SIR DOUGLAS MAWSON in 1910 very nearly joined forces with Captain Scott, but there was so much to be done and Mawson's own plans were of such vast importance that, since funds were forthcoming, it was better to have this great Australian explorer leading and conducting his own expedition.

The first Australian Antarctic expedition was undertaken soon after Scott organized his last expedition. Mawson planned to work Adélie land and connect it properly with South Victoria Land, and alone of all South Polar explorers he achieved all that he had set out to do. He took Captain John King Davis as his second-in-command, and Master of the seasoned whaler *Aurora*. He also had with him Frank Wild, that tough little seaman, who even in civilized lands looked like an Elizabethan : he reminded me of Drake's men and Frobisher's men ; and Chaucer's knights and squires, as I have always pictured them. It may be mentioned that the *Aurora* was so old that she had gone to the relief of the United States General Greely's expedition in 1884. Mawson took with him in this 600-ton weakly-powered veteran vessel 49 Greenland dogs as his principal transport. He fitted his ship with wireless, and communicated constantly with Australia via a W.T. station, which he established on Macquarie Island. He left Hobart on December 2, 1911, a year after Scott had sailed south in the *Terra Nova*, and was soon wallowing in a Southern Ocean gale. After leaving Macquarie Island he was nearly three weeks making Antarctica, then the *Aurora* encountered the ice. New land appeared on January 2, and Mawson's men saw an iceberg which they found to be covered with earth. Two days later a vertical wall of ice was seen. It was found to be trending southwards and they followed in that direction. This proved to be a low barrier attached to a new coast. The ice-cliff rose to a height of 200 feet, and after encountering a typical blizzard which obscured everything from view, a steep snow-clad promontory, rising to 2,000 feet, was seen, and then Mawson's great geographical discoveries commenced, from just within the Antarctic Circle to the south of the D'Urville Sea. New bays and capes were charted at the beginning of 1912, and fairly shallow water, largely ice-free, permitted Mawson to set up his main base at Cape Denison in what he christened Commonwealth Bay. He was disappointed with the featureless nature of the new land, and although he gave his own modern name to what he discovered, it was by Mawson that the name of D'Urville Sea was given in honour of the French explorer who had first sighted Adélie Land, farther to the westward, in the year 1840. Another base was set up under Frank Wild to the westward. Mawson was extremely fortunate in his choice of Hurley as his camera artist. Hurley and Ponting rank as the two great photographers and cinematographers of modern British Antarctic expeditions, and I shall never forget a day spent in company with these two men of genius, looking through their superb illustrations of the Great White South.

It fell to this distinguished Australian explorer, Mawson, to prove the non-existence of certain Antarctic lands that earlier explorers had placed on the very sketchy maps in the possession of the leading geographical societies of Europe and America, notably Sabrina Land and Côte Clarie. Mawson's maps show quite an archipelago, which includes the Mackellar Islands, the Way Islands, Stillwell, Close and Hodgeman Islets. It is considered that Mawson's men faced generally worse weather conditions than any previous expeditions to the South Polar regions. In Mawson's historic book *The Home of the Blizzard*, storms are told of in which quite frequently the wind force exceeded one hundred miles an hour, and his huts were only prevented from being blown away because they were so deeply embedded in snow.

Mawson's Cape Denison party consisted of eighteen men, who built two huts, one to live in and the other to be used as a laboratory and workshop. Besides this, two magnetic huts and a transit house were constructed, and an engine and dynamo were installed. This expedition was remarkable for the heavy snowfall which had the advantage of protecting the huts. There is a delightful little harbour at Cape Denison, almost completely land-locked—one of the few pleasant features of the locality. Hurley, the photographer, made some clever photographs showing men leaning against the wind at incredible angles " the head being level with the hips ", and although Scott and Shackleton both tell of terrible blizzards, their weather conditions were a great deal more comfortable than those experienced by Mawson.

Mawson's sledge journey, with Mertz, a well-known mountaineer and ski-running champion of Switzerland, and Lieutenant Ninnis, is virtually an Antarctic saga. It may be called his Far-Eastern journey, and covered 600 miles out and back. Mawson took seventeen dogs and 1,700 lb. of equipment and supplies. Ascending the continental slope on a south-easterly course to a height of over 2,500 feet, Mawson discovered and helped map two huge glaciers, which he called after Mertz and Ninnis. One of his dogs was lost in a crevasse after four had already been killed, and he nearly lost one of his sledges, which hung in a crevasse but was skilfully recovered. The party had fearful weather, but pushed on, intending if possible to sight Oates Land, which I had named after I succeeded Captain Scott in command of his last expedition. On December 14, 1912, Ninnis fell with his sledge through a snow bridge into a yawning chasm, and was lost. What a tragedy !—the tent had gone and Mawson and Mertz had nothing but a spare tent cover to protect them against the rigours of that awful climate. With the few dogs remaining and no food for them except old furs and scraps, the bereaved pair commenced a race against death and started homeward for Cape Denison. Coming back to an earlier camping ground where a spare sledge had been left, they made tent poles out of its runners, and with six starving dogs, and a meagre supply of sledge rations and kerosene with which to cook dog-flesh and supplement their provisions, they continued towards their base. Mertz was badly frost-bitten, they were cold, and growing rapidly weaker. On January 7 Mertz became delirious, and had several fits. He was obviously dying, and, although Mawson did everything possible, Mertz passed away soon after midnight, leaving his gallant leader alone on the frozen waste. Mawson's outlook was wellnigh hopeless, and two days later he wrote : " There is little chance of my reaching human aid alive." A blizzard held him up next day and another delayed him further. His feet were in shocking condition, but his strong will kept him going. After some awful falls into crevasses, which somehow he managed to get out of, his guardian angel guided him to a mound on which a bag of food had been placed by a search party, which left news that the *Aurora* had returned, after the winter.

Had Mawson reached this point six hours earlier, he could have returned to Cape Denison in time to board the *Aurora*. As it was, after being delayed a week by a blizzard, he got back to Cape Denison just in time to see the ship sailing away ! However, a small party was remaining at the hut, with whom he faced the second winter. This party, which wintered a second time on the bleak coast of Adélie Land, consisted of seven, whose loneliness was enlivened at breakfast-time by wireless news, Mawson being the first British explorer to establish wireless in the Antarctic.

Mawson was fortunate in having Captain J. K. Davis in command of his expeditionary ship, for this well-known Antarctic navigator charted a great deal of new coast-line, sailed over the charted position of earlier explorers' land, found new territory which he named Wilkes Land, so called in honour of the American explorer who voyaged thereabouts in 1840, and on February 1, 1912, in latitude 65° S. and longitude 116° E. he sounded in 927 fathoms, continuing to the westward. A gigantic ice-tongue was discovered and named " Termination Tongue " since its position lay in that assigned by Wilkes to his Termination Land. It was over a hundred miles out of sight of the nearest land.

On February 12 Captain Davis made the important discovery of an open sea which now bears his name. New lands were found, and on February 13 high snow-covered coast-line was observed and subsequently christened " Queen Mary Land ". Near here, Wild's party were disembarked and their base established on the Shackleton ice-shelf seventeen miles from the mainland. Wild had seven companions with whom he spent a somewhat uneventful winter.

However, there was excitement enough to follow, and it is regretted that the nature of this little book does not permit of greater justice being done to Frank Wild and his seven companions.

On March 14, 1912, Frank Wild made a sledge journey to the south where the continental slope rose rapidly to a height of 3,000 feet. After the first day's sledging new land was reached when " numerous crevasses appeared and camp was pitched on the lower slopes of the hills, with magnificent ice-falls on each side ". These were examined next day, then a blizzard kept the party in its tent until noon on March 17. Continuing southward Wild's party camped when 1,400 feet above sea level. From March 18 it took two days to advance nine miles. On the 21st, after marching nearly eight miles farther, Wild reached a height of 2,220 feet and then he was held up by a week's blizzard when the tents became almost buried in snow. Wild's party established a depot at a height of 2,600 feet and then returned to their base, which was reached on April 6.

And now Wild faced truly terrible weather. His wireless masts were erected with great difficulty, but uprooted by the force of the wind in the first blizzard.

On August 22 Wild, with five companions, started on what proved to be one of the worst journeys recorded in the history of Antarctic exploration. This depot-laying journey led eastward over the Shackleton Shelf. A small nunatak (rock peak) was discovered on August 23 and then, after some further progress eastward, more blizzard weather was encountered and the party imprisoned by driving snows.

After discovering some rocky outcrop between Masson and Henderson Islands two more nunataks named the Alligator and the Hippo were charted, the latter being over 400 feet in height. It was of granite on which moss was found growing. The depot was laid near the Hippo nunatak in latitude 66° 25′ S., longitude 98° E. about 85 miles from Wild's base, and on September 4 the depot party turned homeward. On camping after the first day's homeward march at the foot of the Avalanche Rocks (400 feet of rock with 200 feet ice-cap above) a terrific squall blew down both tents and no sooner had they been set up again than an avalanche came down, some of the rocks nearly reaching the tent. Breaking camp next morning, one of the tents was torn from top to bottom by the wind. Then to make themselves secure the party dug a 12 feet deep by 6 feet trench which they roofed with the sledges and the best of the two tents, and here the six men were compelled to remain for five days. The wind force is recorded as exceeding 100 miles per hour, and one of Wild's party, Harrisson, was literally lifted by the wind, clean over Wild's head, and thrown down 20 feet away.

After another blizzard in a temperature of 30 degrees below zero, the base was reached on September 16, 1912.

The western depot party led by Dr. Jones started on September 26, and during this sledge journey it took six days to struggle nineteen miles through blizzard weather. October brought more unspeakable weather with thirteen out of sixteen consecutive days of hard wind and thick drift.

Weather of :

> Blizzard and blow,
> Gust, squall and snow,
> Hazard, discomfort and storm.

And, because of such hardships :

> All that was fun,
> All that was cheer,
> All that was joy was gone.

Wild's little party completed the various explorations made in the first few months of their visit and added a great deal of geological value to our knowledge of ice structure and glaciation. The mighty unknown glacier which was named after Lord Denman, the then Governor-General of Australia, was discovered " rolling in magnificent cascades from a height of 3,000 feet . . ." In this direction he found the ice so honeycombed with pits and chasms that the men felt like flies walking on wire-netting.

Whatever monotony Wild's men felt when they first established their base and faced a dark, lonely winter was made up for by the adventures and surprises met with in the second half of their stay.

Wild was of the Bowers type—tough, hardy and reliable, an ideal second-in-command for any Polar expedition.

Before concluding this chapter on Sir Douglas Mawson's Antarctic expeditions mention should certainly be made of the Magnetic Pole or Southern journey made by Mawson's men in 1912–13.

R. Bage, one of the most active and reliable of Mawson's men, led a Southern sledge party accompanied by Webb and Hurley. Bage's work has been fully described in Mawson's *The Home of the Blizzard* and in C. F. Laseron's *South With Mawson*, and in the back of my mind I have a vivid picture of Bage in company with Webb and that splendid photographic artist Hurley facing weeks, nay months, on the plateau under the most arduous and hazardous conditions. Bage carried out a 600-mile sledge journey taking valuable magnetic observations—it is a story of daily blizzards, bad surfaces, well below zero temperatures, long arduous days, snow blindness, frostbitten fingers and, through their missing a depot, a bitter race for life against the spectre of starvation.

Bage's party on December 21, 1912, recorded a magnetic dip of 89° 43' which told them that they were standing virtually at the South Magnetic Pole.

In Bage's own account of this historic sledge journey he says it became necessary to build " break winds " to protect the tent from the constantly recurring gales, which literally reached hurricane force on occasions. On November 25, 1912, he and his party observed two snow-petrels which " had actually flown 76 miles inland to a height of 2,450 feet. . . . They were a beautiful sight, hovering with outspread wings just above the snow, tipping it with their feet now and then, to poise without a flutter in a 65-mile gale."

Bage's account is most appropriate to a general description of the desolate Antarctic. He describes the scenery in one place as becoming if possible " more desolate ".

This little party were called on by a skua gull when 125 miles from the sea. Hurley supplied a particularly interesting photograph of a truly rough sledging surface of high sastrugi which was encountered by Bage's party when 200 miles S.S.E. of the winter quarters in King George V Land.

When, after passing latitude 73° S. 256 miles from the base, they were travelling at an altitude of 5,500 feet to their surprise they had a heat wave on December 19 and a dead calm. To quote Bage : " The tent became absolutely oppressive. The rime coating the walls inside thawed and water actually trickled into our finnesko (fur boots). . . . We were not used to this sort of thing and struggled out hurriedly for a breath of fresh air."

On December 21 in latitude 70° 36' S., longitude 148° 10' E., at an altitude of 5,900 feet, Bage, Webb and Hurley hoisted the Union Jack and the Commonwealth Ensign and gave three cheers for the King—" Willing, but rather lonesome away out there."

They searched the horizon, but could see nothing but snow undulating in endless sastrugi. Bage reckoned that they were about fifty miles from the South Magnetic Pole itself. They were about 175 miles from the spot where Professor Edgeworth David, Douglas Mawson and Dr. MacKay had stood in 1909 when these three members of Shackleton's 1907 *Nimrod* expedition were the first men to reach the South Magnetic Pole.

This important journey was accomplished in six weeks' outward marching and by this time the party were very short of finnesko, which had moulted badly and were by then " almost bald ".

Fortunately sail was made use of during the return journey and some very good marches made, one run being nearly 42 miles, which meant a surplus in the food ration—a most rare thing in Antarctic sledging. Some bad turns of snow blindness shook them severely, but despite numerous setbacks and very real hardships they won through and caught sight of the Mackellar Islands and reached their hut in the late afternoon on January 11, 1913.

In 1930 Mawson again visited Antarctica and completed his Polar plans by exploring in the vicinity of Enderby Land.

It may be said of Mawson's Expedition that it is credited most justly with having added more geographical and scientific discoveries than any previous Antarctic expedition ; but the work goes on and will go on. The late Gino Watkins in the north, Rymill and Ryder in the south, are type-specimens of what our British Commonwealth of Nations has to show in the youthful British Polar explorers of to-day. How finely, how worthily they have upheld the traditions and the heritage handed down to them by those whose Homeric deeds I have done my best to portray.

Gordon Hayes in his *Conquest of the South Pole* says of Mawson : " Sir Douglas Mawson, apart from being an excellent administrator, bears little resemblance to either of his predecessors. Nature was in a generous mood when she made him, as she was when she built Antarctica. The word 'strength' comprehensively sums up his character both in mind and body, and he almost suggests an incarnation of the South Polar Continent that he has done more than any other explorer to unveil."

This from the scientific standpoint is probably true, although Ross, Scott and Shackleton run him pretty close in their geographical discoveries, and for speed and distance covered plus discovery Amundsen has to be counted in, and so, of course, does Byrd. However, we are as yet only dealing with the desolate Antarctic up to the early twentieth century visitors. This takes us up to the year, say, when the first World War came to an end. British Antarctic explorers handed the torch to Australia,

New Zealand, the United States and Norway (for the last-named captured the best of the whaling industry in the Antarctic, and Amundsen was the first to reach the South Pole).

And now, before including the Antarctic attainments of the man who has frequently been referred to as The Last of the Vikings, and passing on to the Flying Age of South Polar Exploration, may I say that last year, 1948, when I re-visited the sea-girt continent Australia, I met not only Sir Douglas Mawson and Captain J. K. Davis but Captain Doorly, to whom I have already referred, and the members of the Australian Antarctic Club, several of whom had wintered at Cape Denison and sledged over Adélie Land and King George V Land, and men who were working out the programme of the Australian Government for making use of the meteorological and hydrographical and magnetic knowledge acquired in the Australian and New Zealand sectors of Antarctica. Indeed one and a half million pounds have been voted by the Commonwealth Government for Antarctic exploration and the Committee responsible for administering this vast sum contains able experienced and imaginative Australians, who have the Commonwealth interests and civilization's well-being at heart. I believe and hope that the Australian Antarctic Exploration Committee's President is Sir Douglas Mawson himself.

Unfortunately I did not meet Rymill, that go-ahead young South Australian leader of the Graham Land Expedition of 1934–37, but no doubt his Antarctic knowledge will be made available where necessary.

The present Australian Antarctic expedition is under the command of Group Captain F. A. C. Campbell, R.A.A.F., and is engaged in the geological exploration of the Australian Antarctic quadrant.

Australia is maintaining two very important meteorological, hydrographic and magnetic stations on Heard Island and Macquarie.

Captain J. K. Davis, who is now director of Navigation for the Australian Commonwealth, was as alive and alert in matters connected with the Antarctic Ocean as in dear old Shackleton's days. I told him of my last meeting with Commander Wild and we discussed the risks he took when he established himself on " Queen Mary Land ". After five days Commander Wild's party of eight, having got their " base " transported to the top of the ice-cliff by means of a flying fox, had said " good-bye " to Captain Davis and those on board *Aurora*, and to quote Captain Davis " When at 7 a.m. on the 21st February, 1912, they all scrambled over the rail with their blankets on their backs, we wondered when we sailed away whether we should find them there when we returned the following year."

One could write here a great deal about the indomitable little Wild and the exciting details of his rescue, and it should be recorded that Mawson's folk experienced a wind velocity of 116 miles per hour, which is probably the highest ever reported from a meteorological station. As Wild told me, when I last saw him in Johannesburg, Mawson certainly discovered the windiest country in the world !

Chapter Nine

ROALD AMUNDSEN

FIVE hundred years before Christopher Columbus discovered America, Leif Erikssen with a number of Vikings (and Valkyries) landed on the North American Continent, and it only seems fitting that that modern Viking, Captain Roald Amundsen, first to make the North-West Passage and one of the crew of the *Belgica*, the first ship ever to winter in the Antarctic, should be the first man to reach the South Pole and secure for the Norwegian nation the honour of that achievement.

Amundsen, during his famous Arctic voyage of 1904–6 in the little motor schooner *Gjøa*, re-located the North Magnetic Pole and very considerably added to our knowledge of the Arctic.

Amundsen's conquest of the South Pole was justly spoken of by Sir Clements Markham, Scott's special champion, thus : " It was a miracle of forethought and organization, the success of which was aided by remarkably favourable weather and no doubt also by the fact that the explorers were all practised ski-runners."

Having been lent Nansen's old ship the *Fram* and acquired the best ski-runners, dog drivers and ice pilots obtainable, ninety-seven eskimo dogs and a sufficiency of the Nansen-type sledges, Amundsen sailed on August 9, 1910, provisioned for two years.

Calling at Madeira on September 6, he announced his plans and sent a cable to Captain Scott, which was received on board the *Terra Nova* in Melbourne and which read : " Beg leave inform you proceeding Antarctic Amundsen."

The *Fram* had been re-rigged as a fore-topsail schooner

and often made ten knots speed without using her motor. Beyond sighting Tristan da Cunha and Kerguelen Island no land was seen before the Great Ice Barrier was reached.

The *Fram* was berthed in the Bay of Whales and unloading commenced forthwith.

The dogs were worked in two shifts to land stores, huts and equipment. The Norwegians, nine in number, who had been chosen to form the shore party sledged the stores over the two miles of frozen sea. This work and the building of Amundsen's hut took only a fortnight and on January 27, 1911, the shore party " moved in ".

On February 3 the *Terra Nova*, as already stated, arrived in the Bay of Whales with Lieutenant Victor Campbell's party on board.

The two explorers exchanged calls and Amundsen invited Campbell to winter alongside of him, but Campbell, having seen that the ice conditions off the coast of King Edward VII Land were insuperable, and having found the *Fram* in his next choice for winter station, decided to seek winter quarters elsewhere. As we know, he spent a winter at Cape Adare, and a second at Terra Nova Bay much farther south.

Now, concentrating almost entirely on the attainment of the Pole, Amundsen's first depot party left " Framheim ", as he called his winter-quarters, on February 9 and in four days reached latitude 80° S. almost one hundred miles south of the base in longitude 153° 45′ W. The Barrier surface was found so suitable hereabouts that the dogs came back in two days at an average speed of fifty miles a day !

The second depot journey started off with eight men, seven sledges and forty-two dogs, passing the first depot, and conveying a load of over one thousand pounds to latitude 81°. Three men turned back here on March 4, and the other five pushed on to 82° and left 1,250 lb. of stores on March 7, and then returned to Framheim.

A third depot journey was undertaken when a ton of seal meat and 400 lb. of other stores were taken to the first depot. By April 10 no less than 7,500 lb. weight had been laid out in the three depots.

Roald Amundsen accompanied all these depot-laying parties.

With this knowledge the Norsemen faced the winter with equanimity. They then set to work to improve the sledging equipment and reduce the weight of the sledges. The weight-saving was almost incredible.

Tents were provided for the dogs even, and provision made to feed them, mainly on seal meat of which nearly sixty tons were available. Huge boots were made for the Polar party, who wore no less than six pairs of socks or stockings to save frost-bite.

The winter of 1911 may be reckoned from, say, April 21 to August 21 and the position of Amundsen's winter quarters is given as 78° 36' S. 153° 45' W.

Framheim was soon snowed under, but the little party were experts in carpentry and all the trades that mattered in that ice-bound community. Cold it certainly was, but not windy like Adélie Land.

According to Helmer Hanssen (for whose book *Voyages of a Modern Viking* I wrote a special foreword in 1936) : " There was quite a little tent-town on Framheim. The dogs alone numbered 117 ; we had to have 8 tents for them and then there were all the tents for provisions, clothing and equipment."

One man invented a ski-binding with hooks which could easily be unhooked and brought into the tent at night so that the dogs should not eat the leather !

Amundsen made it a rule for everyone to have steady regular work.

It was to Bjaaland and Stubberud that the expedition owed the reduction of the weights of the heavy sledges from about 150 lb. to *scarcely more than* 60 ! Wisting and Hanssen did the binding work on the sledges. This was indeed an art which they excelled in. Pigskin thongs were used and the sledges, in spite of the strains to which they were subjected and the rough handling they endured with about 900 lb. weight on them, were almost as good after the Polar journey as they were when they left winter-quarters.

Wisting was the tailor to the party—in fact he was to Amundsen's expedition what Petty Officer Edgar Evans was to the Scott expedition.

Lieutenant Prestrud, afterwards Norwegian Naval Attaché in London, was the astronomer. Johansen looked after the provisions and also packed them. He was outstanding in his ability to fit and stow compactly.

As to Amundsen himself, Hanssen writes of him :

> Amundsen as leader had to undertake all calculations as well as personally inspecting all the work done by others. He was first man out every morning. He always found something to keep us all interested in. For instance, when he had taken the temperature every morning, he had us all guess how cold it had been during the night. He carefully noted each man's guess and at the end of the month he took each man's average and the one who was nearest to the average shown by the instruments received a prize. These prizes were not cheap stuff. I remember one got a silver watch, another books and so on. Finally, we got so trained that we had only to stick our noses out of doors in order to tell to a degree how cold it was,

Of Lindstrøm, who was the cook, Hanssen says :

> His cooking got better and better . . . the course we all considered the world's best was simply hot cakes with sugar and marmalade, and to the end of my days I shall see before me Lindstrøm standing at the end of the table, comfortable and round, while four of us at each side of the table sat expectant like hungry young birds in a nest, waiting for the hot cakes he dealt to each from the tower in front of him.

Lindstrøm was left in charge of the base and kept the

meteorological records while the other eight were away sledging. He was indeed a favourite and a philosopher ; he was also superstitious and protested vigorously at the South Polar trip setting out on a Friday, and begged the men taking part to wait until Saturday.

Anyway on a Friday far too early in the spring the first journey began. The bitter cold was too much for dogs and men and after several days with temperatures as low as minus 72°, or 104° of frost, the sledge loads were placed at the first depot in 80° and the party returned to Framheim, to be greeted with the cheerful jeers of the Jeremiah-like prophet, Lindstrøm.

Nevertheless, the Polar party started off on a Friday, October 20, when Lindstrøm again prophesied disaster.

The party consisted of Amundsen, Hanssen, Wisting, Hassel and Bjaaland, with four dog sledges and the fifty-two best dogs. The loads were light enough in view of stores for four months being already laid out in the depots at 80°, 81° and 82°.

According to Amundsen's reckoning, the distance from Framheim to the Pole—as the Skua flies—was 684 geographical miles, or nearly 770 statute miles, which meant that Amundsen had only to average about fifteen miles per day to remain on full rations throughout the long cold trail, and, since the loads were reasonably light for the type and weight of dogs employed, *the men on ski were dragged along as well, right up to latitude 85°*—nearly 350 miles ! Contrast this with my own sledge party who were compelled to pull their own sledge for 1,500 miles.

With the exception of crevasses which appeared in certain areas, the Barrier stage was fairly uneventful. On November 8 in latitude 83° land was sighted to the south-westward and from then onwards new land, new mountains and glaciers were constantly appearing above the horizon to the south-west, south and south-east.

Amundsen found that the Barrier surface continued

" excellent ". New depots were left at every degree of latitude.

Latitude 84° was reached on November 12, and on the 16th in latitude 85° 5' S., after crossing huge undulations, some as much as 300 feet in height, land was reached and " No. 6 depot established 930 feet above sea level ". Here sixty days' provisions were taken on, while a thirty-days supply was left, that is, enough to take the party back to Framheim under easy steam.

A five or six mile reconnaissance was now made, and when two thousand feet up bare rock was seen and geological specimens obtained.

Hanssen writing of the outward journey says :

> For us humans driving to the South Pole regions was just like play, but it was no fun for the dogs. They had to be driven hard and whipped if we were ever to get there, in fact. If there is any truth in the doctrine of transmigration of souls, I sincerely hope my next incarnation will not take the form of a dog on a Polar expedition.

Hanssen's account of the Polar sledge journey is very readable ; it is written with the sailor's simplicity, just a straightforward narrative with no striving for effect, but one learns quite a lot from it, for instance he says that the dog-drivers always kept a tight hold on a rope tied on to the sledge—frequently men or dogs fell into crevasses. The dogs were held by their harness, suspended in mid air with the blue-black inkiness of unfathomable depth below them, and in the case of the men they had to be alert, very alert, for they had not the sledging harness which Scott's and Shackleton's sledge-haulers wore and which kept them secure. It is very comforting to feel the strong belt and shoulder straps holding you up when you are down a crevasse, and a shower of ice and snow descends on you.

Amundsen's team had a most unpleasant experience after climbing a big hill—the Norsemen found that it was a glacier badly criss-crossed with crevasses. It sounded hollow when they commenced walking across it. Fog came on and as they could not see to find their way round the hill they were compelled to stay the night there. They named it the Devil's Dance Hall, but, as Hanssen says : " Such an incident, however, is just like a patch of bad weather on a ship's voyage ; it is no sooner over than it is forgotten, leaving behind it only a feeling of gratitude at having escaped."

Now Amundsen's party satisfied themselves with fifteen geographical mile marches daily. To their surprise, the temperature became milder and milder, although they were ten or eleven thousand feet up.

When they passed 88° 23', which was Shackleton's farthest south, Amundsen stopped and hoisted his flag in honour of Sir Ernest Shackleton and his comrades. Amundsen has often told of this tribute and stated his unbounded admiration for that terrific Polar sledge journey.

And now, within one hundred miles of the uttermost south, the goal of their hopes, dogs and men were in first-class condition, their daily observations agreed exactly with the distances shown on their sledge meter, and when, according to Hanssen's calculations, they had only five nautical miles to go, he stopped his dog team, unharnessed one of his dogs and let him run alongside. " Then I called out to Amundsen to come on and run ahead."

" Why should I ? " asked Amundsen.

" I cannot make the dogs run without someone running ahead," said Hanssen.

Then when the five miles had been run, he called out to his leader again that they must be at the Pole.

The four sledges stopped, and on that exciting yet solemn occasion Amundsen, as always, thinking of his comrades, made each of them hold the bamboo flag-pole, with the Norwegian flag flying from it, as it was forced downward into the snow.

The refinements of hourly observations showed that the party were still five miles away from the South Pole itself, and, after spending the night where they had planted the flag, they moved on next day to the Pole itself. The position was actually fixed by means of two sextants, and artificial horizons. Scott used one of our little four-inch sledging theodolites, and it is a fact that the two explorers' fixing of the position of the South Pole differed by not more than one scale division of the theodolite, half a mile at the most! So there was no doubt about it.

The Norwegians had brought with them a small light brown silk tent, which they fixed and left standing on the pole. In this they placed a few articles of unwanted clothing, one of the sextants and an artificial horizon.

Amundsen left a letter in the tent addressed to the King of Norway and also a letter to Captain Scott, whom he was quite sure would be at the Pole sooner or later.

On arrival at the Pole Amundsen said : "If I know the British rightly, they will never give up once they have started, unless forced by something beyond their control. They are too tough and stubborn for that."

The details of Amundsen's return journey have been published fully. The greatest enemy was fog—and there is fog in those Antarctic highlands. And fog can be a very unpleasant customer when looking for a depot, as Amundsen found, for when his team got back to the glacier named the Devil's Dance Hall, thick weather came on which made it impossible for them to see a hundred yards. Camping for the night and searching again in the morning found them unsuccessful, and so they camped once more, to wait for the weather to clear. After a while the fog lifted enough for Amundsen to get a glimpse of the way he wanted to go. Nevertheless, although they struck camp and harnessed the dogs and started off, the fog descended once more, the weather became darkly overcast and the depot was never found, despite a two-day search.

With only one day's sledging ration left, the valiant Norseman took a great risk. He asked his companions "What do you think? Hadn't we better let this depot go and push on to the next whilst we still have sufficient food left?"

When thirteen miles north of the Devil's Dance Hall Hanssen, looking back, recognized the view they had all seen on the outward way when two deep crevasses, one on each side of their route, were identified by all. Now the weather was clear enough to make it almost certain that the missing depot could easily be found. Amundsen thought it was too far to drive back, since they had now got so far towards the next depot, and that it would be wiser to go on. However, Bjaaland, who a few years previously had been Norwegian ski-champion, was enthusiastic to go back with empty sledges after Hanssen had invited him, and back the two men went. They reached the missing depot after driving eighteen miles, ate some chocolate and gave a double pemmican ration to the dogs, filled up with the cached provisions and got back to the party after driving most of the night and doing a ten-hour sledge run on top of their work of the previous day. They had driven fifty-six nautical miles in the twenty-four hours, i.e., sixty-three statute miles.

Hanssen modestly states that "In Alaska on good and hard snow I have driven sixty nautical miles, which equals 111 kilometres, in twelve hours. But with half-starved dogs, and in such a country, I do believe this twenty-four hours' driving constitutes a record."

After that they came back at a splendid speed. Amundsen left the South Pole on December 17, 1911, and reached Framheim on January 28, 1912, at four o'clock in the morning. He was certainly a cool customer—entering the winter-quarters he found Lindstrøm and three companions fast asleep, woke up Lindstrøm and said " Good morning, my dear Lindstrøm, have you got some coffee for us ? " Lindstrøm sat up, and rubbed his eyes. " Oh, is it you ? " he said, " I thought it was the Japs," to which Amundsen replied " You didn't want us to start on a Friday, but not only did we start on a Friday, but we came back on one too." I like Helmer Hanssen's remarks : " After 99 days of cocoa that coffee was delicious. There would have been a funeral in Framheim if we had been offered cocoa. It was good to be alive when we had got our pipes going. When we got back we were not reduced in weight, but had even put on flesh. Amundsen's splendid planning and careful preparations, and the endurance of our dogs, had turned the trip into a picnic. As we sat in comfort that day at Framheim we thought about Scott and his comrades, whom we felt certain would reach the Pole."

Apart from what I have written and quoted there are some descriptions of Amundsen's sledge travelling with his admirable dog teams, and also of Prestrud's work in the direction of King Edward VII Land. Prestrud also brought back to Framheim some geological specimens, but in view of Commander Byrd's Little America Expedition which largely threw the whole Continent of Antarctica on to the screen, I will do no more than mention the Prestrud shelf-ice, which this Norwegian naval officer charted and added to the Ross Sea quadrant, and mention the Japanese Antarctic expedition before enlarging upon ice, blizzards and calms—three of the most important components of this desolate little-known area.

Of Japanese efforts there isn't much to be said. Amundsen has something to say about the *Kainan Maru's* visit to Framheim, and Prestrud says that the Japs seemed to be a lot of healthy, well set up little men. Lieutenant Shirase, their leader in the 1910–12 Japanese expedition, drew up a programme which intended ten men to be landed with ten Manchurian ponies in Mc-Murdo Sound. Five Japs were to march to the Pole. The other five were to lay out depots to ensure their return. However, although the *Kainan Maru* left Japan in November, 1910, she did not even reach the Ross Sea, and returned to Japan in May, 1911, having failed to achieve anything worth writing about.

In 1912 the *Kainan Maru* reached the Bay of Whales on January 15, to find the *Fram* awaiting Amundsen's return from the South Pole.

The Norwegians visited the Jap ship, and witnessed what they called *Slagtningen av de Uskyldige* (the slaughter of the innocents!) referring to the wholesale and un-necessarily brutal killing of penguins and seals.

Homura, Captain of the *Kainan Maru*, visited the *Fram*, and after leaving four men in a tent on the Barrier, left for King Edward VII Land, with a view to dis-embarking there. Two of the Japanese made a sledge journey south-eastwards across the Great Ice Barrier, reaching 80° 5′ S. in longitude 156° 27′ W. where they found the ice to be 1,000 feet above sea level. This, as far as I can see, was the only bit of geographical work carried out. Little else was attempted.

The first time I had the pleasure of meeting Roald Amundsen was in Christchurch, New Zealand, when he came to see me early in 1912, while I was recovering from my severe attack of scurvy. His account of meeting the Japanese was full of humour, and he described the occasion of Prestrud's surprising two Japs while they were " investigating " the contents of a depot which had been laid out by the Norwegians. Caught in the act, the Japs hurriedly hid what they had in their hands behind their backs, and one of them with a mischievous, schoolboy-like grin, looking around at the featureless waste of snow, said " Plentee ice ".

There certainly was!

99   H 2

Chapter Ten

EXPLORING ANTARCTICA

Now that Antarctic visitors, who include whalers, sealers, explorers, film operators, and the armed forces of powers conducting exercises in connection with a " cold war ", have run into thousands, it is hardly possible to mention every Antarctic leader. Amundsen and Scott both drove their arrows into the lifeless heart of the desolate Antarctic. Byrd looked down upon it, and all three of these men and those who accompanied them and supported them drew aside the ice-bediamonded veil that had hidden for countless thousands of years the innermost secrets of the Antarctic Continent.

Of the early twentieth century visitors, a Frenchman, Dr. Jean Charcot, whom Scott described as " the gentleman of the Pole ", carried out between 1908 and 1910 his second expedition to Antarctica, following that which he commanded in the little *Français* five years earlier, when he wintered in the ice near Wandel Island (or Booth Island) which is *not* in the Antarctic, being in latitude 65° S., and carried out some sledging and added to De Gerlache's work

Charcot had a beautiful little barque-rigged auxiliary vessel *Pourquoi-Pas*, built for him, and in this ship he again wintered off Petermann Island—which is scarcely ten miles to the south-westward of the winter-quarters of the *Français* and not, to Charcot's disappointment, nearly within the Antarctic Circle.

Dr. Charcot settled down to serious scientific work at the beginning of February, 1909. Four huts were erected for magnetic observation and atmospheric electricity, for seismograph and for a transit instrument, all of them being lit by electricity. An efficient meteorological screen and tide gauges were set up as well. Some sledging and boat journeys were carried out, which have mostly been described in Charcot's picturesque English in his beautifully illustrated book *The Voyage of the Why-Not in the Antarctic*.

Charcot and some of his crew suffered from scurvy and ophthalmia. For the latter, Charcot strongly advocated yellow glasses in place of the smoked glasses commonly in use in the early nineteen hundreds.

Jean Charcot, besides being a great gentleman, was a great philosopher : he said (realizing that it is an advantage that each man should have a cabin or some such place to shut himself in) : " It is often more difficult to bear the daily pinpricks than the great griefs."

And being a Frenchman he has a great deal to say about food and meals. When lecturing in Paris in 1914 and 1920, I visited Charcot, and we had a great deal to talk about. He was full of humour and tremendously pro-English, but he always shook his head about English cooking. His idea was that when, during the French Revolution, hundreds of French chefs invaded England they brought their art with them, but the English cooks never could acquire the refinements of French cuisine. I believe it was Charcot who told me the story of the old French chef who worked in a New York Club until he decided to retire on his seventy-fifth birthday and return to his home in Avignon to end his days in true comfort on the fortune he had amassed in the States. The President and Committee of the Club, conscious as they were of the debt they owed to the old gentleman, decided to give him a farewell banquet. It was indeed a banquet worthy of a prince, and Monsieur " Ratatouille ", as we will call him, was truly a prince among chefs, and the dinner, the wines, the atmosphere and the speeches were worthy of the occasion. Finally, the President of the Club—a well-known banker—presented Monsieur " Ratatouille " with a golden casket, containing a cheque for twenty-five thousand dollars. At the end of the President's speech—which included all the tributes that the Prince of Chefs would like to have paid to him—with a faint vein of humour, the President said " And now, in wishing you continued health, happiness and all that you wish yourself in your retirement, we, the members of this Club, are going to ask you to bequeath to us the secret which you have so carefully kept—the secret of your ' savoury omelette ' which no other living chef can serve up as you have done." Amidst roars of applause the President sat down and Monsieur " Ratatouille " arose and, stroking his pointed beard, and blushing, literally blushing in his happiness despite the lump in his throat, said : " My friends, my dear generous friends, I can find no words sufficient to thank you for this dinner, for your splendid gift, and for your real friendship. Sixty years ago, my father bequeathed the secret of the savoury omelette to me and I have kept it. Now, I will tell it. It is very simple—even more simple than Columbus's secret of making an egg stand on end—it is just this. Anyone can make a savoury omelette. You don't even have to be a chef to do that. But when the omelette is about to be taken to the table you take a shallot, bite 'im—bite off the end—and breathe right on to the omelette 'on keep the fragrant parfum just long enough for the first opounful of omelette to reach the mouth."

Dr. Charcot, to my great joy, commanded a mine-sweeping trawler in the Dover Patrol during World War I and won the D.S.C., of which he was very proud.

His greatest Antarctic discovery was Charcot Land, which he named after his father, Professor Charcot, an outstanding French savant.

Poor Charcot is no more. He lost his life when in his beloved *Pourquoi-Pas*, which was wrecked on the Icelandic coast and dashed to pieces in a storm.

Charcot loved poetry and in exchange for my *Keeping the Seas* he wrote the lines I said I liked in my French version of his book :

April 1.

> *Avril vient de naître*
> *Et par la fenêtre*
> *Le soleil joyeux*
> *Nous fait les doux yeux*

Jean Charcot, nearly fifty years ago, spent some time with Scott, Skelton and Michael Barne doing trials of motor sledges and he co-operated with my own grand leader in every possible way.

And now, Drygalski and Filchner who also helped frame the Antarctic Continent. Erich von Drygalski and Lieutenant Dr. Filchner were, I suppose, disciples of Dr. Karl Fricker, whose work *The Antarctic Regions* was translated and published by Swan Sonnenschein & Co. in London as far back as 1900. Both Fricker and Hugh Robert Mill pay great tribute to Professor Georg von Neumayer for his efforts to promote the despatch of a purely scientific expedition to the Antarctic, ever since that eminent scientist went himself to Australia in 1856 to fit up and direct the Flagstaff Observatory, Melbourne, erected for the study of meteorology, terrestrial magnetism and hydrography.

Neumayer's unwearying efforts were supported and continued by Baron Nordenskjöld, famous already for his circumnavigation of Asia. Nordenskjöld planned also a voyage to the Southern Seas, which, through financial stringency, he was prevented from making. But the plans were there and his aspirations were carried out by the eminent German scientist, Erich von Drygalski, whose expeditionary ship the *Gauss*, a wooden barquentine built on the lines of the *Fram*, wintered in 1902 near a peak named by this expedition " Gaussberg " in Kaiser Wilhelm II Land, almost on the Antarctic Circle.

Drygalski's men built an observatory entirely out of ice-blocks, and with German thoroughness carried out their winter station duties and also some sledging. Like Scott, Drygalski had taken a captive balloon with him, and on March 29 he made an ascent to 1,500 feet, sighting a 1,000 foot high black, steep-sided mountain and also the ice-clad Kaiser Wilhelm II Land extending many miles to the east and west.

Drygalski, like Mawson, experienced tempestuous winds for a week at a time. He undertook more sledging in the spring, rather for research than for geographical exploration.

On February 8, 1903, the ship began to be freed from her icy home, and after a two-months' struggle in heavy pack ice she worked clear and made her way back to Cape Town.

For some unaccountable reason Germany failed to support her Antarctic scientific ventures ; it seems to me that the Junkers looked down on the scientists, and certainly those German scientists who invented the gyroscope compass had little love for the Junkers !

Drygalski was a contemporary of Scott in his first expedition, and Lieutenant Filchner of Scott and Amundsen in 1911. Captain Scott with his usual foresight made a strong point of including scientists from the British Commonwealth outside of the British Isles in his British Antarctic Expedition of 1910-13, and so we had Griffith Taylor, Frank Debenham and Raymond Priestley from Australia, Charles Wright from Canada, and, if one likes to stretch a point, Simpson from India, and Bowers from the Royal Indian Marine—and I include Lieutenant H. R. Bowers, for, with his truly scientific mind, he was more than a scientist in embryo.

Most of the Dominion scientists had been to Germany, and all of them paid tribute to the German scientists who had looked upon the Antarctic as of vital importance to science.

Dr. Karl Fricker put German efforts in their proper perspective, and our scientists were very generous about their German confrères.

War with Germany was on the horizon when I went to Berlin to lecture to their Geographical Society, and for that reason my acquaintanceship with Filchner never developed into real friendship. It was difficult to get his expedition story until after the Second World War!

The second German Antarctic Expeditionary ship, which took Filchner south, was the wooden whaler *Björnen* (whose name was changed to *Deutschland*), a vessel on which many of us had cast covetous eyes, notably Lieutenant Michael Barne, who had planned a joint expedition with me, to leave in 1909 and work to the eastward of King Edward VII Land, but sufficient funds were not forthcoming soon enough and when Scott announced his plans for his last expedition, Michael Barne and I immediately stood aside, cancelled our plan, and devoted our efforts to helping the British Antarctic Expedition of 1910–13. *Björnen* was a little too small for Scott's expedition.

The *Deutschland* sailed from Hamburg on May 3, 1911, via Buenos Aires and South Georgia, to the Weddell Sea. She carried a crew of thirty-five, including five scientists and two surgeons. Twelve Manchurian ponies and two Greenland dog-teams were embarked.

Unfortunately Filchner suffered badly from sea-sickness, and was further handicapped by the ill-health of Captain Vahsel, who subsequently died on August 8, 1912, from rheumatism and general debility. He was buried in the Antarctic.

During the sub-Antarctic part of the voyage, a storm was encountered and Filchner records waves sixty-five feet in height. One can well believe this, after making this passage eight times as I have done, and after comparing notes with other exploring ships' commanders and navigators.

Filchner pushed southward fairly rapidly, but by December 17 the pack-ice had become formidable and the ship was held up until January 24, 1912, when the ice loosened and the *Deutschland* continued southward well into the Weddell Sea. Soundings showed that the expedition was nearing the continental shelf. Weddell's farthest south, latitude 74° 15', was passed on January 29, and next day land was sighted—magnificent ice-cliffs 150 feet in height, to seaward, behind which the Antarctic continent showed itself rising gradually to about 2,000 feet covered by heavy ice-cap.

All this Filchner described enthusiastically to Captain Amundsen and myself when in January, 1914, he and I were the guests of the valiant Norseman in Berlin. This new land was christened Prince Regent Luitpold Land.

The coast was followed for two days when a bay was entered in 77° 45' S., very similar to the Bay of Whales of the Ross Barrier. The height of the ice-cliffs was about sixty feet thereabouts.

After February 18 the bay disappeared due to an extraordinary spring tide, ocean swell and blizzard. A full description of the breaking up of the Barrier here appears in Filchner's book.

From what he told, there was a big tabular berg aground in Vahsel Bay on which it was decided to land ponies, sledges and stores, and erect the hut they had brought south

All this work was carried out in fine weather, and less than a fortnight later came one of those unexpected calamities when bergs twenty miles long break off barriers and ice-shelves and drift away to sea.

In this particular break-up, most of the stores were salved, as were the hut and transport animals, except for one dog that went to sea on the berg. The *Deutschland* surrounded by heavy pack was carried northward, and, unable to work free, drifted through ten degrees of latitude during a winter captivity, and emerged from the

ice-pack in latitude 63° whence she made her way back
to South Georgia and thence to Germany.

Filchner, who had made plans for a further season's
work, was discouraged or forbidden to continue his
exploration and his expedition was therefore only partly
successful.

However, he had shown great courage and made a
ninety-four-mile sledge journey in the pack-ice, in which
he proved the non-existence of land reported by Morrell
named after him Morrell Land, or New South Greenland. This journey was in mid-winter. Two dog-teams
were employed. A sounding of 600 fathoms gave " no
bottom " and proved that Morrell Land did not exist,
anyway in the position given by the American captain
in 1823.

The lowest temperature on this sledge journey was
minus 34·6° Fahr. ; the minimum temperature recorded
by the *Deutschland* was minus 48° Fahr. on July 13, 1912.

During the Antarctic summer season, 1929–30, Consul
Lars Christensen sent the *Norvegia* (Captain Nils Larsen)
on a new expedition, commanded by the naval airman
Captain Riiser-Larsen, to examine the coast and explore
between Kemp Land and Coats Land, from the air, and
also to find new whaling grounds, and undertake a
series of scientific investigations.

Norvegia carried two planes and Riiser-Larsen had
with him Captain Finn Lutzow-Holm, as pilot, and also
two air mechanics.

Before leaving Norway, Riiser-Larsen received a
special authorization from the Norwegian Government
to take possession of any new land that he might dis-
cover for the Norwegian crown.

One of the reasons why Lars Christensen chose the
Kemp Land (Enderby Land)—Coats Land stretch,
which the *Norvegia* had already visited in 1927–28, was
to avoid clashing with Mawson's plans, observing that
Sir Douglas had decided to operate in his old field in

the Eastern Antarctic, whilst Sir Hubert Wilkins had published his intention of continuing his exploration in Western Antarctica.

In volume III of Bjarne Aagaard's *Fangst og Forskning i Sydishavet* is a map, which shows the overlapping routes of the Mawson and Norwegian expeditions of 1930–31 to the Antarctic. The names given to the newly discovered features are differentiated according to their origin. This map contains an inset giving the full track of Mawson's expeditionary ship from Tasmania over the position of Emerald Island, which does not exist, thence to the Balleny Islands, King George V Land, along the coast of Wilkes Land to Enderby Land, and back to Tasmania. On the main map Mawson's expedition's flights together with the tracks of the *Torlyn* and the *Thorshavn* are shown.

Reference to the general chart of the Antarctic given at the front of this book will demonstrate that Riiser-Larsen had a very wide field to work in, which extended through eighty degrees of longitude.

From my knowledge of Riiser-Larsen and of Sir Douglas Mawson I feel that the redoubtable yet modest Mawson would fix up with the gallant and fair-play-loving Riiser-Larsen to the mutual satisfaction of both Australia and Norway, and, although both explorers at times gave different names to capes, headlands, peaks and banks, the work of the *Discovery* Committee in the Sub-Antarctic Zone and in the Antarctic waters and on the continent itself has correlated Mawson's, Wilkins', Riiser-Larsen's and Byrd's exploration results better, far better than has been the case with early Antarctic discoveries.

The millionaire shipowner, Lars Christensen, has been most altruistic and public-spirited in connection with research and exploration in the Southern Seas, and on the desolate Antarctic Continent. The achievements of his whaling fleet, and the experiences of those who have sailed under his flag, would fill several volumes, and if I were to write a history of the Antarctic I could find almost half of the facts and the things that matter in Bjarne Aagaard's three encyclopædia-like, beautifully illustrated books which contain better detailed maps than any other publication.

Chapter Eleven

ICE, BLIZZARDS AND CALM

O NE of the reasons why there can never be an accurate chart of the Antarctic is because of the constantly changing barriers, which form such a large part of the coastline.

In the *Terra Nova* on her way south, an ice island was sighted thirty-one miles in length, which was estimated to be of about the same surface area as that of the Isle of Wight, or about 150 square miles. And there are innumerable instances of exploring ships sighting gargantuan icebergs. The *Scotia* sighted an ice island of similar size, and in 1892 in the South Atlantic in 43° S., longitude 33° W., an island of snow and ice, more than forty miles in length, was seen.

The Weddell Sea ice barrier, the Ross barrier, the Wilhelm II Land barrier and others which are the crystal ramparts to the ice-capped continent all change their shape and limits, as witness Byrd's discovery of the total disappearance of Framheim and a large portion of the Bay of Whales, when he established his Little America Base on the Great Ice Barrier in 1929. Scott found in October, 1911, a couple of miles of Erebus glacier tongue had broken off which had turned through a half circle, the old western end pointing east.

The photographs and sketches which illustrate the countless books, diaries, magazine articles and reports which have been published on the subject of the Antarctic would literally take many months or even years to study, and ice-pictures depicting pack-ice, pancake ice, ice-sculptures, brash-ice, freshwater-ice, firn-ice, sea-ice, bay-ice, avenue-ice, ice-bastions, ice-floes, icebergs, ice-shelves, bottleglass-ice, piecrust-ice, inland-ice, pin-nacled-ice, ice-crystals, ice-islands, ice-caps and ice-plateaux, ice-barriers and so forth would fill many, many books.

Ice structure and glaciation is a science by itself. I believe that Captain Scott and Dr. Wilson were the first to think of appointing a special member of a Polar expedition to make a study of this interesting subject.

" Silas " Wright—now Sir Charles Seymour Wright, K.C.B., O.B.E., M.C., F.R.S., M.A., Chief of the Royal Naval Scientific Service, was *our* ice expert in Scott's last expedition.

Griffith Taylor, Wright, Debenham and Evans' western geological journey in January–February, 1911, is well worth reading. " Griff " has great literary ability. He describes the Koettlitz Glacier and its ice-pinnacles which are nearly 100 feet high. He also mentions coming across two seals " asleep as usual " on the old glacier ice more than twenty miles from the sea.

Wright and Debenham, later, both tell of meeting " parties of seals " thirty miles from the sea on the Koettlitz Glacier. The ice-crystals which they photographed on the roof of a cave near the head of this glacier resembled pine twigs and were two inches long. They found here " many brownish ice stalactites and stalagmites " and Charles Wright was in his element.

Concerning ice barriers, Scott's and Shackleton's people consider the Great Ice Barrier to be an enormous sheet of floating ice of probably 600 feet average depth. And as you could put the whole of Great Britain and Eire on it, its area must be over 120,000 square miles. Personally, I do not believe that the *whole* of the Great Ice Barrier is afloat, but I bow to the majority who do !

One thing is certain, that the land ice in Antarctica largely preponderates over the sea-ice, whereas the opposite is the case in the Arctic.

What strikes the newcomer to the Antarctic is the

icing-sugar-like whiteness of the icebergs and ice-islands, and also the peculiar stratification of the bergs and their undulating white strata.

In the *Challenger* reports, 1874, forms of icebergs are included, which seem almost unbelievable but the sketches are dated and come from the most reliable source, and so can be counted on as *seen*—but it must be remembered that most of the bergs were seen north of the Antarctic Circle, which was only crossed on February 16, 1874, in longitude 78° 22′ E., when the *Challenger* penetrated eight miles into the Antarctic Seas and re-crossed, I believe, within twenty-four hours.

Sir Charles Wright, like Professor Griffith Taylor, has the gift of clear language, and his *Notes on Ice Physics* in *Scott's Last Expedition* are well worth reading. He points out that the climates of the earth are almost entirely controlled by water in one of its three forms. Wright, likewise, draws attention to the fact that the rigidity of freshwater-ice is far far greater than that of sea-ice. He says " As a result ice even four or more inches thick is for sledging by no means safe, whereas the same thickness of freshwater-ice would be sufficient to support a regiment of soldiers".

How true this is. There is a lake six miles long below the place where I am writing this book. I have seen a motor tractor go across it to-day on ice only three and a half inches thick, whereas the sea ice where our best motor sludge broke through on " black Sunday", January 8, 1911, was quite three times as thick.

What a blessing it was for Scott's last expedition that Wright had the support of Griff and Deb., and Griff had the support of Deb. and Wright, and Deb. had the support of Wright and Griff, for these three were a triptych whose combined efforts would indeed have delighted poor Scott and Wilson had they lived to see the works of these young energetic Australian-Canadian scientists published in their entirety.

One thing that is obvious to most students and experts in the behaviour of floating ice-masses is that due to more ice being submerged than there is above the sea surface, icebergs, ice-islands and ice-floes are at the mercy of ocean currents and even tidal streams rather than under control of the winds.

It has even been suggested by the German, Dr. Karl Fricker, that "under favourable circumstances this phenomenon—that the path pursued by the berg must depend mainly on the direction of the prevailing oceanic currents—might be utilized to observe the deep-sea currents ; for since an iceberg like every other floating body must direct its line of gravity parallel to the impelling currents, the longitudinal axis of the berg must indicate the constant currents prevailing beneath the changing currents on the surface ". What a mouthful !

Captain J. G. S. Doorly, writing in his diary when third officer of the relief ship *Morning*, notes that a line of heavy floes and some small bergs, in spite of the prevailing south-east winds in McMurdo Sound, were propelled by some under-surface current right into the Sound dead against the wind, and says that it was quite uncanny to watch these heavy floating masses working to windward. He adds that the relief ships received some nasty jars lying unsheltered against the solid field-ice. " At times the severe pressure buckled our stout beams a few inches and we were thankful when the dangerous motion ceased."

Fricker suggests that the submerged part of the average berg is six-sevenths of the total depth or height. In the little *Morning* Captain Colbeck considered only about two-thirds of the average berg was submerged.

Colbeck was a very careful observer and a constructive thinker. It was he whose careful and trustworthy map of the Great Ice Barrier showed that its edge had receded about thirty miles since Ross's voyage.

Wright showed that the actual northward movement of the Barrier was about 300 feet in the year.

Half-way through the twentieth century—well on in the Flying Age of exploration—tremendous developments in speed and travel give the physicists and ice experts far finer opportunities even than Wright had, and the gleaming ice-crystals portrayed by Admiral Byrd's photographers make one realize that the siege of the South Pole has been followed by conquest, and that with the advent of the modern ice-breaker, like Byrd's *Northwind,* even the insuperable pack-ice that kept Lieutenant Victor Campbell from landing on King Edward VII Land is no longer impenetrable.

Blizzards. Speaking generally the worst blizzards seem to have been encountered by Mawson, although that nine-day blizzard on the Great Ice Barrier which brought about the death of Scott, Wilson and Bowers when they were only eleven miles south of One Ton Depot will always be looked upon as the cruellest blizzard in the history of the Antarctic.

That terrible blizzard! On Thursday, March 29, 1912, Scott managed very painfully to write " . . . every day we have been ready to start for our depot 11 miles away, but outside the door of the tent it remains a scene of whirling drift. . . . It seems a pity but I do not think I can write more "

Blizzard and drift in the Antarctic—the thoughts of them make me shiver as I write in this snowbound hut in the Norwegian mountains, where I have spent so many happy weeks with my little family, and where in the long light summer days my grandchildren now come with their parents. To-night, March 5, with a log fire burning in the big open hearth and a peasant woman as cook—one who really can cook—my wife and I have looked up in *Scott's Last Expedition* 5th March, 1912, and we find :

Monday, March 5. Lunch. Regret to say going from bad to worse. We got a slant of wind yesterday afternoon, and going on 5 hours we converted our wretched morning run of 3½ miles into something over 9. We went to bed on a cup of cocoa and pemmican solid with the chill off. The result is telling on all, but mainly on Oates, whose feet are in a wretched condition. One swelled up tremendously last night and he is very lame this morning. We started march on tea and pemmican as last night—we pretend to prefer the pemmican this way. Marched for 5 hours this morning over a slightly better surface, covered with high moundy sastrugi. Sledge capsized twice ; we pulled on foot, covering about 5½ miles. We are two pony marches and 4 miles about from our depot. Our fuel dreadfully low and the poor Soldier nearly done. It is pathetic enough because we can do nothing for him ; more hot food might do a little, but only a little, I fear. We none of us expected these terribly low temperatures, and of the rest of us Wilson is feeling them most ; mainly I fear from his self-sacrificing devotion in doctoring Oates' feet. We cannot help each other, each has enough to do to take care of himself. We get cold on the march when the trudging is heavy and the wind pierces our warm garments. The others, all of them, are unendingly cheerful when in the tent. We mean to see the game through with the proper spirit, but it's tough work to be pulling harder than we ever pulled in our lives for long hours, and to feel that the progress is so slow. One can only say " God help us ! " and plod on our weary way, cold and very miserable, though outwardly cheerful. We talk of all sorts of subjects in the tent, not much of food now since we decided to take the risk of running a full ration. We simply couldn't go hungry at this time.

Reading on, I came to :

the weather conditions are awful, and our gear gets steadily more icy and difficult to manage. . . . But the wind came from the WNW as we broke camp. It rapidly grew in strength. After travelling a half an hour I saw that none of us could go on facing such conditions. We were forced to camp and are spending the rest of the day in a comfortless blizzard camp, wind quite foul. . . .

Yes, blizzard is public enemy No. 1 as far as the Antarctic explorer is concerned, and yet in every expedition I have had to do with " the bliz " is the subject on which most of the Antarctic jokes are made.

In Scott's first expedition when only Captain Armitage, Bernacchi and Koettlitz had had any Polar experience the efforts in short sledge journeys were very amateurish, and as Scott put it " Tuesday, March 11th (1902) was to be one of our blackest days in the Antarctic. . . ." It was that day that a blizzard developed, and a small party in great discomfort left their tent and endeavoured to return to the greater comfort of the ship in her winter-quarters.

With no real blizzard experience, and no knowledge of the ease with which one can get completely lost in the drifting snow, Able Seaman Vince was whirled down a steep, slippery slope into the bay north of Hut Point, behind which *Discovery* was anchored. He must have been killed in a matter of a few seconds. In my youthful diary I wrote when two years later the *Discovery* was freed from her winter-quarters behind Hut Point : " Our united efforts were crowned with success. Our great wish was realized, and the three ships left in company. A strong gale blew till the evening of our departure, and we made some sail to start with. As the night wore on, we watched the great snowclad mountains grow smaller and smaller, and one could hardly repress a shudder at the thought of the terrible loneliness in which we were leaving a little cross, ' Sacred to the Memory of Able-Seaman G. Vince, R.N.'—a solitary grim record of a life lost, a sacrifice to the *relentless blizzard*, which we had come to know so well."

The loss of poor Seaman Vince was an object lesson which Scott and all *Discovery's* officers drove home in such a way that neither Shackleton's nor Scott's people ran any unnecessary risks—the one exception being in mid-winter, July, 1911, when our enthusiastic naval surgeon, E. L. Atkinson, during a blizzard, with a temperature of nearly 30 degrees below zero, made an attempt to read one of our outlying thermometers, not very far from the main hut at Cape Evans. It was only a mile away, but for some unaccountable reason he missed the thermometer, went past it and was lost in the driving snow. It was not until 2 a.m. next day that all the search parties got back and Atkinson was rescued. There is a picture showing his badly blistered frost-bitten hand and another showing Petty Officer Evans binding it up. These are facing page 344 of *Scott's Last Expedition*, volume I, and a couple of pages earlier are Scott's comments, " It is a rambling tale to-night, and a half thawed brain ", etc. Scott winds up with : " Yet it is impossible not to realize that this bit of experience has done more than all the talking I could have ever accomplished to bring home to our people the dangers of a *blizzard*."

Yet we continued to make jokes about blizzards, and so did Shackleton's folk and Mawson's men, and so we know did the Norsemen, and no doubt others too.

When Shackleton was preparing for his great southern journey, he was so full of enthusiasm that he hardly allowed his men to cease work even in bad weather, much less because it was Sunday !

Day, our motor engineer, told me when he was work-ing with our motor sledges about dragging stores for the southern journey from Cape Royds to the foot of the Barrier. The wind was increasing, it was blowing twenty-five miles per hour one Sunday forenoon, and frostbite was playing about fingers and faces, whilst Shackleton in the hut was putting the finishing touches to his instructions and plans. Several times his chaps had gone in and reminded him that the wind was increas-ing, that there were signs of a blizzard approaching, and that it was getting very cold, and threatening. Shackle-ton looked up from his work, nodded, and even smiled.

The wind blew harder and harder until "the crowd" felt that they must indeed protest. Day was deputed to go in and protest. And this is what happened : Day, with his balaclava helmet all frosted up, and a cake of ice on his muzzle, said "It's blizzing, Boss, the wind's increasing, dark snowclouds are working up, and some of us are getting frostbitten." Shackleton smiled benignly, turned up a passage in the Bible which lay on his table and handed it to Day. "Read that," he said. Day read aloud "Many are called, but few are chosen." "Read it again," said Shackleton. Then he shut the book and looked quite sternly at Day, but with the faintest gleam of humour in his eye, and exclaimed "Many are cold, but few are frozen."

Once only in my lifetime have I had cause to thank God for a blizzard, a three-day blizzard on that bleak inland plateau that surrounds the South Pole.

Soon after saying good-bye to Captain Scott and his companions in 87° 35' S., when we knew that we must use our greatest possible efforts to make northing to get on to the Beardmore and thence down to the Great Ice Barrier, and on for another five hundred miles, we were overtaken by a blizzard which lasted three days. Normally we should have camped and waited until it abated and the weather was again fit for sledging, but the wind, blowing hard from the southward, made it possible for us to drive northward with the floor-cloth of our tent set ao a oail. We sped forward like a small boat driven before a gale, and made amazing progress, as I have told elsewhere. That blizzard is one that I shall never forget, because it certainly saved our lives.

The trouble about these blizzards is in the impossibility of predicting them. They frequently come on without warning, and perhaps the threatening appearance of weather results in angry-looking clouds dispersing as quietly as a Channel mist on a September morn, like one gets on the Belgian coast.

Dr. Simpson—" Sunny Jim " or Professor Sir George C. Simpson, K.C.B., C.B.E., F.R.S., D.Sc.—I imagine could write a whole book on blizzards, and when he joined Scott he had already spent a winter in the Arctic. He points out that great cold without winds is much easier to bear than a much higher temperature with winds ; in Polar exploration the wind is the chief enemy, not the cold and the blizzard. " Hard wind and driving snow " is the arch-enemy.

We had, as already stated, far more blizzards than Amundsen.

Simpson states definitely that the blizzards which have been so fatal to British Antarctic exploration are local winds confined to the western half of the Ross Barrier. This is a very important statement.

In 1909 I took to show to Scott the circular which I had had printed with plans for the proposed expedition with Lieutenant Michael Barne, already referred to, and our base was to have been the Bay of Whales—Scott himself agreed to make his base there, but he was persuaded on the principle that " the devil you know is better than the devil you don't know " to make his winter-quarters in McMurdo Strait.

Amundsen was, of course, the first explorer to make a long sledge journey across the Great Ice Barrier, well away from the land, and when reading Simpson's meteorological report, and also those of Mawson and Shackleton, one realizes why the fortunes of Antarctic sledge parties have been so largely affected by the weather. And what's more, one is forced to realize that my late leader had far more than his share of blizzards and setbacks due to unusually bad weather. The same can *certainly* be said of Mawson.

Calms. Thank God there are calms in the desolate Antarctic. There are calms on the Great Ice Barrier, and on the Beardmore Glacier too, but seldom, if ever, on the plateau. And, thank God, there are occasional calms in the Antarctic Seas. I can plainly remember two. The first was early in January, 1903, when after a three-day hurricane the wind fell light and we made all plane sail. The sky cleared and we sighted the high mountains of South Victoria Land—great rugged peaks, Mts. Adams, Sabine and Minto. Gradually the banks of stratus cloud, which had clothed the distant peaks when first we saw them, disappeared and for four hours I gazed spellbound at this vast wondrous land of ice and mystery, in which we hoped to find Captain Scott and his fellow-explorers. A gentle swell remained to remind us of the storm we had come through. The ship rolled and a flap of the sails told me we were becalmed. In my boyish diary, I say :

. . . As the day drew on the land appeared still more plainly, and everyone became excited for in its grandeur it was beyond our wildest expectations.

We admired the huge, snow-clad mountain ranges, and we steered our ship amongst tabular icebergs that were so awful in their greatness that our small exploring vessel gave one the impression of a toy. One can scarcely conceive what immense pieces of ice they were—over 400 feet in height some of them, and a mile long.

It was all so splendidly organized by Nature that day. The clouds rolled back like a theatre curtain, and dispersed into wispy sheets of fluff, and then before us spread a magnificent panorama of glistening white and blue.

We passed a great deal of compact land ice too, with whole armies of penguins in occupation, some resting, some basking in the sun, and others diving and splashing about like a happy holiday crowd.

" Clinkety-clonk, clinkety-clonk, clinkety-clonk " came the metallic beat of our obsolete engine up through the open hatch—poof-f-f-f ! spouted a whale right alongside of us ; gaw-awk, gaw-awk, gawk ! squawked the penguins clustered on the floe ; coo-oo-oo-ee shouted Gerald Doorly and I to get the echo back from those majestic-looking

Seals basking on the floe-ice off Cape Evans.

On the next two pages :
The *Terra Nova*.

The *Terra Nova* seen from a grotto in the ice.

bergs, and all the world was gay. Down below in the forecastle the seamen eating their breakfast in their watch below heard the coo-oo-oo-ee, looked at one another, grinned half-contemptuously, for they knew who it was —the ship's two greatest enthusiasts—" Mad ! " they said, but they put down their mugs, left their mess stools and came up and looked, all the same.[1]

The other calm that is indelibly stamped on my memory was in January, 1913, when in command of the *Terra Nova* I was making my way down to McMurdo Sound, as I thought, to embark Scott and the main landing party at Cape Evans. In my book *South With Scott*, I have set down my impressions :

The evening before we finally broke through into open water was beautifully still, and a low cloud settled down in the form of a thick fog—it was a change from the fine clear weather—frost rime settled everywhere and for a time we had to stop. There was a weird stillness over all, and whenever the ship was moved amongst the ice-floes a curious hiss was heard ; this sound is well known to all ice-navigators, it is the sear of the floe against the green-heart sheathing which protects the little ship, and it is to the ice-master what the strange smell of the China Seas is to the Far-Eastern navigator, what the Mediterranean " cheesy odours " and the Eucalyptus scents of Australia are to the P. and O. officers, and what the pungent peat-smoke of Ireland is to the North Atlantic seamen. I suppose the memory of the pack-ice hissing around a wooden ship is one of the little voices that call—and they sometimes call as the memory of a " tall ship and a star to steer her by " calls John Masefield's seamen " down to the sea again ".

I sometimes feel a mute fool at race meetings, society dinner parties and dances, the lure of the little voices I know then at its strongest. It is felt by the Polar explorer in peace-times and in the hey-day of prosperity, and it is surely that which called Scott away, when he had everything that

[1] From *Adventurous Life*, published by Hutchinson.

man wants, and made him write as he lay nobly dying out there in the snowy wilds :

" How much better has this all been than lounging in too great comfort at home."

Dr. Rudmose Brown, a veteran Polar explorer, in his *The Polar Regions*, says when talking of Antarctic anti-cyclones :

The high pressure over the continent gives rise to the prevailing southerly winds that blow off the continent, generally with an easterly component due to deflection by the earth's rotation, but sometimes with a westerly compo-nent, the latter perhaps the result of local topography. They blow normally with the strength of gales with inter-mittent blizzards which all south polar expeditions have experienced. On Adélie Land, D. Mawson recorded wind velocities of 80, 90 and even 116 miles an hour. The average wind velocity for the year was 50 against an average in Europe of 10 miles an hour. Such also were the blizzards with which Scott and Shackleton had to contend on their Polar journeys over the high plateau.

Lastly, in confirmation of this air circulation over the ice-cap are the observations that the upper air currents feeding the anticyclone are more or less opposed in direc-tion to the surface ones. This has been shown by the use of balloons, and is seen in the direction of clouds and the smoke of the lofty volcano of Erebus.

On the equatorial side of the Antarctic anticyclone pressure is low, and gulfs of low pressure extend from the Southern Ocean into the Ross, Bellingshausen and Weddell Seas, giving rise to clockwise winds which lead to the peculiar distribution of ice in those seas. In latitude 83° S. the Scott expedition experienced in midsummer a northerly blizzard with temperatures as high as 33° F. due to a vast low-pressure area over the Ross Sea. . . . This belt of raging winds and storm-tossed seas must be traversed by every Antarctic exploring ship, as many a deep-laden vessel has proved to its cost.

Yes, the sailor and the scientist agree in most things,

especially in meteorological things, concerning the desolate Antarctic and the waters surrounding that continent.

Rudmose Brown has a good deal to say about ice and blizzards, but not much to say about calms.

As far back as 1861 an eminent Scottish scientist, Sir John Richardson, LL.D. wrote a book on the Polar Regions, but the first three hundred and fifty pages (Part I) are taken up with ice, winds and currents of the Arctic, whereas Part II contains only thirty pages about the Antarctic, and even in that, space is taken for islands well north of the Antarctic Circle.

Lars Christensen, to whom I refer elsewhere in this book, in his work *Such is the Antarctic* gives what he calls " the impressions of a greatly interested spectator who has seen the wonders and the glory of the mighty Antarctic Ocean in her various moods, in her fury and in her indescribable calmness and beauty ".

Fortunately Miss Jayne, an English girl who lives in the Viking Country, has made an admirable translation of Consul Lars Christensen's manuscript, which has been published by Hodder & Stoughton. He, Lars Christensen, includes a whole chapter on what he refers to as " The Norwegian Mainland ", which is to my mind a valuable historical and geographical contribution from one who has frequently seen it and whose name has been given to an important stretch of Antarctic coastline lying between 50° and 70° E. longitude.

From *Such is the Antarctic* we find that the first man to set foot upon the soil of Antarctica was a Norwegian, H. J. Bull, who on February 24, 1895, landed at Cape Adare.

Lars Christensen has probably done more for whaling than any man living, besides picking on an outstanding naval-airman, now Admiral Riiser-Larsen, who really rediscovered Enderby Land in 1929, and subsequently discovered Queen Maud Land, Crown-Princess Martha Land, Princess Ragnhild Land, etc.

This " Norwegian Mainland " was partly charted by Lars Christensen's ships and aircraft. I believe this enterprising and influential Norwegian shipowner was the first to use aircraft for tracking whales in the Antarctic. One of the seaplanes used by the *Norvegia* he christened *Qarrtsiluni*, which is Eskimo for the " soul of a whale ". But the seaplane actually used for the Norwegians' most important Antarctic discoveries was a Hansa-Brandenburg reconnoitring plane, built in Norway, and lent by the Norwegian Navy for Riiser-Larsen and Lutzow-Holm's flights. Its official name was *F.18*.

Lars Christensen has the blood of a sailor and a Viking coursing through his veins, he understands that ice, wind and weather are the things that matter most in the whaling industry, and what is more he has cruised in his own ships a great deal in the Antarctic Ocean, which is most encouraging to his captains, officers and men. He adds to that encouragement by taking Mrs. Lars Christensen with him.

Norwegian claims to the mainland, already referred to, have been very nicely defined by a prominent Australian statesman—I call him a statesman because he is a great deal more than a politician. Mr. Casey said : " Norway is now and has always been in the forefront of the exploitation of whaling throughout the world, and now in the Antarctic. Norway is by far the greatest individual factor in the world's whaling industry. It can be taken for granted that Norwegian interests in whaling in the Antarctic will in no way suffer because of the action of the Commonwealth in acquiring sovereignty over this large sector."

This was in 1933 when the British Antarctic chart showed MacRobertson Land (after the Australian Antarctic Expedition's survey) and the Norwegian map showed Lars Christensen Land—both being the same land.

There are still indications of a British-Australian-Norwegian Antarctic *Entente Cordiale*—long may it remain.

Incidentally there are still disbelievers in the story of Jonah and the Whale—but however small the whale's mouth may be, there is a splendid photograph in *Such is the Antarctic* showing a whale, killed by electricity, lying on the deck of the *Solglimt* with its jaws wide open, inside of which can be seen four of the ship's crew with Lars Christensen in the foreground, and, as humour is the prelude to friendship, I trust that since both our nations have such a keen sense of humour, they will remain friends for ever.

Chapter Twelve

MODERN EXPLORATION

IT fell to Sir Hubert Wilkins, that enterprising Australian explorer, to introduce flying into the desolate Antarctic, where he had already been for a short time with Mr. J. L. Cope, with a view to charting the western coastline of the Weddell Sea in January, 1921.

At the end of 1928 on the shores of the big land-locked harbour of Deception Island, Wilkins found a landing ground for aircraft, and made it his base. In one of his two seaplanes, *San Francisco*, Wilkins, with Lieutenant Eielson as his co-pilot in the Wilkins-Hearst Expedition, flew from this base and found Graham Land (as he says) to be an island about 350 miles long and of an average width of nearly forty miles, with a horizontal summit 8,000 feet above sea level. From the *San Francisco* it was a wonderful view, and the islands and outcrops from the barriers could be seen, also long and narrow fjords, inlets and ice-filled bights, nunataks and plateaux.

The Lockheed mountains were discovered and also Stefansson Strait, which was something like a hundred miles in length and almost thirty miles wide, likewise Casey Channel named after the distinguished Australian member of the Federal Parliament, and also Crane Channel which is as big or even bigger than Casey Channel. In this flight Sir Hubert Wilkins reached latitude 71° 20' S., longitude 64° 15' W. flying over a new stretch of land, which he took to be a part of the Antarctic Continent, and which he named Hearst Land.

Wilkins made another flight on January 10, 1929, over

Charcot's bases on Wandel and Petermann Islands. Apart from the foregoing, he flew almost across Graham Land from west to east, and on February 1, 1930, flew from the edge of the pack-ice in 70° S. 101° W. and reached 73° S., finding only pack-ice which he believed to be fast to the mainland farther south.

And now, before turning the South Polar searchlight on to Byrd, and giving some idea of his vast achievements in Antarctica, let us look at that splendid, modest and able Polar explorer, Lincoln Ellsworth. Twice he attempted to fly right across the desolate Antarctic, unfortunately without succeeding; but on his third attempt, in company with Mr. Hollick Kenyon, he achieved his purpose, and bridged Antarctica for the first time, making four landings between Cape Eielson and the Bay of Whales.

Lincoln Ellsworth was a veteran Polar flier and his adventures in the Arctic alone would fill a book, but it was not really until Sir Hubert Wilkins in the Antarctic summer of 1928–29 flew along the coast of Graham Land that he appears to have had Antarctic aspirations. Realizing that the desolate Antarctic was a land mass almost as large as North America, and, from the airman's view-point, almost an unknown land mass, he had a meeting with Wilkins and got to know him and appreciate his adventurous nature and capabilities. Enlisting Sir Hubert Wilkins' aid he planned a bold " leisurely crossing ", which included coming down for surface observations and for camping if need be during bad weather.

Byrd's old ship, the *Wyatt Earp*, was purchased, a crew and scientific staff engaged, and the *Polar Star* was loaded on board in time to make a start from Norway to New Zealand in July, 1933.

At Dunedin, Ellsworth met Wilkins, Balchen, Braathen, and Lanz, his second-in-command, principal pilot engine-mechanic and radio-operator, and the captain, officers and crew of the little *Wyatt Earp*—most of them veteran Norwegian whalers who had been in the Ross Sea before.

The *Wyatt Earp* was only 135 feet long, twelve feet shorter than the *Morning* but of considerably lighter draught. She pushed her way through 450 miles of pack-ice, and on January 9, 1934, moored to the edge of the frozen sea in the Bay of Whales, where the *Polar Star* was hoisted out and dragged a mile in on to the ice.

Very soon afterwards the bay ice commenced to break up and became a grinding mass of floes. The plane was very nearly destroyed. Its ski and hull were crushed and split, and only the wings were left holding what remained of the *Polar Star* out of the Ross Sea. As Lincoln Ellsworth says : " The *Polar Star* was swung aboard, a pitiful sight, skis fractured, one wing bent, unflyable. The expedition was off for that year at least. Only a factory could put the aeroplane back into condition."

Making their way somewhat sorrowfully back to New Zealand, Lincoln Ellsworth's men shipped the battered *Polar Star* on board an oil tanker which was shortly leaving for California.

A fresh start was made and Ellsworth re-cast his entire plan for the projected flight.

Eventually he took off from Dundee Island in the north-east part of Graham Land on November 24, 1935, and flew down over the east coast of Graham Land for ten degrees of latitude, rising to an altitude of 13,000 feet (which is almost the height of Mount Erebus) sighting in Hearst Land a great mountain range " with peaks bare of snow, rising to 12,000 feet above the sea ".

There was a great deal of bad luck attached to Ellsworth's Antarctic venture. The *Wyatt Earp* rolled and wallowed at seven knots from New Zealand to Deception Island to the south-westward of the South Shetlands, and after so many setbacks, misfortunes and breakdowns that there seemed to be some foul spirit stalking Ellsworth and all those who sailed and flew with him, it's surprising that from the moment this great mountain range was sighted everything changed for the better.

On page 300 of Ellsworth's book, *Beyond Horizons*, he writes :

In the clear air we could now see the mountains in all their sublimity. It falls to the lot of few men to view land not previously beheld by human eyes, and it was with a feeling of keen curiosity not unmingled with awe that we gazed ahead at the great range across which our route lay. . . . Suddenly I felt supremely happy for my share in the opportunity to unveil the last continent in human history.

We were indeed the first intruding mortals in this age-old region, and looking down on the mighty peaks I thought of eternity and man's insignificance. So these first new mountains we saw will, I hope, in the future bear the name Eternity Range.

On our long slant it took us three hours to cross the range. I thanked my stars now that I had given myself instruction and training in mountain photography with the Leica, for I had magnificent opportunities which it would have been a crime to muff. Actually, I took thirty-one snapshots of the Eternities, and nearly every one was excellent. The system lay in three parallel ranges divided by high plateaux. Mounts Faith, Hope and Charity were in the middle range. Strikingly contrasted to these rugged Hearst Land mountains were the low-topped Graham Land ranges we had followed south, which dwindled down into isolated peaks as they neared Stefansson Strait. Undoubtedly both ranges are of sedimentary origin. The Hearst Land mountains—at least that section over which we flew —were a loosely-formed range with none of the crowded topography of peaks with glacier-filled valleys and high-crevassed bottoms such as pictures of the Queen Maud Range show. We saw neither glaciers nor crevassed surfaces in crossing.

On we went, the mighty panorama of the Antarctic continent unrolling before our eyes. At the end of three hours the mountains beneath us gave place to a great polar ice plateau from which emerged a few nunataks, the last evidence of the mountain chain we had just passed. We were flying at an altitude of 10,000 feet.

About this time Kenyon noted in his log : " Beginning to fly hands off." This gives an idea of the serenity of conditions.

When still 950 miles from their destination their wireless broke down and left the *Polar Star* droning along a mile above an unbroken desert of snow. Half an hour later, Ellsworth wrote in his diary : " No landmarks visible. Only a limitless expanse of white." More than 100 miles further flying, and then a solitary little mountain range with peaks rising to 13,000 feet— all clustered into a central mass, which dwindled down to merge with the plain around. Its central peak Ellsworth named " Mount Mary Louise Ulmer ", after his wife.

Yes, this desolate Antarctic ; another long black flat-topped range extending through " at least one degree of latitude. This appeared to be the last of the mountains we were to see, for ahead and around swept only a vast plateau meeting the horizon in a vista of white. Throughout the journey, so far, visibility has been from 120 to 150 miles ".

At last after thirteen hours on the wing flying from Dundee Island, they saw what they took to be a water sky, but this vanished and gave way to cloud ! When they had been in the air nearly fourteen hours and had flown over 1,000 miles of continuous mountains and visibility was getting poor, Lincoln Ellsworth and his truly reliable companion, Kenyon, determined to land and take an observation, for they had no petrol to spare !

The account of this flight shows that the two men's

names should be inscribed high on the honour roll of Polar airmen.

When they landed on the cold plateau, they fixed their position, not without a good deal of trouble, as in latitude 79° 12′ S., longitude 104° 10′ W., still 670 miles from the Bay of Whales. Ellsworth says : " We stood in the heart of the only unclaimed land in the Antarctic—in the whole world." He adds : " I felt a very meek and reverent person . . . so here I raised the American flag." He called the area " James W. Ellsworth Land " after his father and that part of the plateau above 6,000 feet he called "Hollick Kenyon " Plateau after his valiant pilot.

The two men remained in Camp 1, as they called it, for nineteen hours, taking observations at three-hour intervals.

The speed of the *Polar Star* had disappointed them, averaging little more than two-thirds of what they had expected.

When eventually they were forced to abandon the plane sixteen miles from the Bay of Whales, they had had another succession of irritating setbacks and mechanical breakdowns, which would have tried Job's patience far beyond breaking-point. Blizzard and consequent delay, threatened frostbite and some gems in humour, as Lincoln Ellsworth's disgusted entry in his diary : " God forbid this aeroplane stuff anyway." But, as he wrote in his book *Beyond Horizons*, " There we were—two lone human beings on an ice-capped continent, the size of North America. . . . We flew over crevasses for about an hour, at the end of which time the surface elevation was about one thousand feet . . ." and later he writes : " Next instant, our fuel tanks completely out of petrol, the propeller was flopping without power. Hollick Kenyon picked his spot; and at 10.03 a.m., local time, December 5, the *Polar Star*, like a weary bird, came gently to earth."

But Lincoln Ellsworth and Hollick Kenyon had crossed the Antarctic from the Weddell Sea to the Ross Sea—a distance of something like 3,000 miles !

When on Sunday, December 15, 1935, the end of the twenty-third day since the *Polar Star* left Dundee Island, Lincoln Ellsworth and Hollick Kenyon let themselves down into a glass skylight which they broke and found themselves in the radio hut of Little America, Ellsworth produced two small bottles of Napoleon brandy given him by his beautiful wife, and celebrated his crossing of Antarctica, tasting the best-ever brandy—brown, fiery, yet smooth as velvet.

Yes, there is still adventure to be had and for variety of adventure give me the desolate Antarctic.

The flight from Dundee Island led to the east side of Graham Land, across the Eternity Range, over the 6,400 foot high Hollick Kenyon Plateau where no less than three landings were made, thence over Marie Byrd Land. A fourth landing was made in latitude 79° 29' S. longitude 153° 27' W. and thence to a position a few miles south of Little America, where in the Bay of Whales Ellsworth and Hollick Kenyon were picked up by *Discovery II* (which had volunteered to take part in the search, and had arrived in the Bay of Whales only just before the *Wyatt Earp*), after wireless breakdown had made Sir Hubert Wilkins believe that they had perished.

The *Polar Star's* position was not apparently fixed.

Chapter Thirteen

ADMIRAL BYRD, WINGED EXPLORER

IN 1930 the American Geographical Society published an account of *The Work of the Byrd Antarctic Expedition* and a year later Putnam's produced Admiral Byrd's *Little America*.

Most of those interested in the Antarctic are no doubt eagerly awaiting the detailed accounts of last year's winged invasion of the South Polar Continent by the United States Fighting Services.

When I have read these and seen the film called *The Secret Land*, I shall feel like the President of the French Geographical Society did at La Sorbonne when he introduced me before my lecture on Captain Scott's last Antarctic expedition, and say to my splendid American confrère: "*Je vais vous donner la parole*", for by then the desolate Antarctic will have, in a sense, been conquered, and we who visited the Southern Continent at the beginning of the twentieth century will willingly take a back seat and gladly see Youth at the Helm!

Rear-Admiral Richard Evelyn Byrd, a Virginian born in 1888, is undoubtedly the greatest of all winged explorers who have visited the South Polar regions. With two ships, the *City* (ex *Samson* of Tromsø), a modern vessel of about 500 tons, and the *Eleanor Bolling*, an iron ship of 800 tons, with eighty-three men and, to my mind, the best outfit any Antarctic expedition has yet been supplied with, Byrd left New Zealand late in 1928. He reached the edge of the pack-ice on December 10, and here had 90 tons of coal transferred to the *City* from the *Eleanor Bolling* which ship then returned to New Zealand. On December 15 the whaler *Larsen* met the *City* at an appointed rendezvous in 67° 48' S. 178° E. and towed her through the ice.

On December 29, Byrd's expedition reached the Bay of Whales where 100 magnificent sledge dogs were landed. On New Year's Day, 1929, the base position was chosen, about eight miles from the Barrier edge, and the unloading commenced.

Byrd appropriately named this base station "Little America" and, from its description, it was by far the most extensive and self-contained of all Polar explorers' bases hitherto established on the Antarctic Continent. The landing party consisted of forty-two men.

Three monoplanes were placed on the Barrier, fitted with ski under-carriages; a huge three-engined Ford with a seven-ton load capacity, a Fokker and a Fairchild. Byrd also had with him a Ford snowmobile.

The detailed descriptions of the Byrd Antarctic expedition published by the American Geographical Society and in Byrd's own book, *Little America*, tell of the twentieth-century revolution in Antarctic exploration. Byrd's successful wireless arrangements are an example of true American efficiency.

The most surprising results were obtained from Byrd's dog-teams, which covered double the distance and dragged well over twice the weight-per-dog that Scott's Siberian sledge-teams managed.

Little America's construction marked a new era in Antarctic exploration. His party led an almost civilized life rather than the backwoodsman kind of existence of previous Antarctics. The chronicler of Antarctic exploration, J. Gordon Hayes, speaks of the three tall radio masts, looking " like the derricks of an oil town. Three main structures were erected : the administration building, in which Byrd and the scientists lived, 200 yards from the other houses as some defence against fire ; the mess-hall—the abode of fourteen men ; and the Norwegian house, originally intended for the machine-shop and only 14 feet long and 11 feet wide. The wireless laboratory and a library of 3,000 volumes were in the first of these buildings. Numerous other little cabins and igloos were constructed and connected by a network of tunnels in the snowdrifts. This winter station had the latest improvements for Polar service, with cold-resisting walls, water laid on from a snow melter, a gymnasium, telephones and other amenities of civilization ".

Byrd's first flight, which was made at a speed of 120 miles per hour, was to the north-eastward. Byrd was accompanied by a pilot and W/T operator and proceeded for 200 miles along the Barrier and parallel to the coast of King Edward VII Land ; a new bay was discovered and the land was then seen to consist of undulating snow-capped country, with fearful crevasses. Beyond Scott's nunatak new land was seen falling rapidly in terraces scored by crevasses from the Alexandra Mountains to the Ross Sea. This journey was made in the Fairchild machine, which on emerging from a heavy snow-squall showed what Byrd described as " a group of highly individualistic mountains ".

These were approximately 1,700 feet in height and lay roughly west by south for fifty miles or so from the Scott nunatak. Byrd counted up to fourteen different peaks, but, his fuel supply running short, he was compelled to return to Little America.

He named the new discovery the Rockefeller Mountains.

On reaching the Barrier edge, Byrd saw that the *Bolling* had secured alongside the *City*. After shifting berth to a convenient position alongside the Barrier face, the *Bolling* was nearly sunk by a fall of ice on her decks. However, her crew after some hazardous experiences got her cargo unloaded, and she sailed again for New Zealand on February 2, 1929.

Her further adventures would fill a fairly large volume,

for she nearly capsized in a hurricane met with on the return voyage whilst in ballast. Nevertheless, she made no less than five complete voyages between New Zealand and the Ross Sea, crossing the Antarctic Circle ten times in all. All of these voyages were only as stormy as Ross had found, and Scott and Shackleton and Colbeck in the little *Morning*, and as I had found when in command of the *Terra Nova*—but the *Bolling's* crew were largely *volunteers serving without pay*.

But, to continue with the landing party, or rather the Barrier party—Byrd's second-in-command and chief of his scientific staff was Dr. Laurence M. Gould, his third-in-command was Captain Ashley McKinley, who was also aeronautical surveyor, and transport officer, while Balchen, the outstanding airman and veteran Polar-pilot, was his principal flying officer.

More exploratory flights were undertaken before the epic flight to the South Pole.

On February 18 the Fokker and the Fairchild machines made further subsidiary flights to the eastward and then to the south-eastward over the Rockefeller range, which was found to contain certainly twenty-five peaks, some of them showing rocky cliffs and outcrops. The Great Ice Barrier stretched away to the southward end of this range. Byrd flew as far as 79° 30' S. and named the new land, which he had sighted near the Rockefeller Mountains, after Captain Scott.

Captain McKinley flew over Byrd's air route immediately afterwards, and made a photographic survey, being directed from the W/T room of the *City*.

Both Byrd and McKinley sighted a high peak, which they called the " Antarctic Matterhorn ", but this appears to have been obscured by clouds before it could be accurately plotted. It is in approximately 151° W. and about the same latitude as Hut Point.

Dr. Gould on March 7, 1929, made a geological journey to the Rockefeller Mountains, with two companions in the Fokker machine, which was unfortunately wrecked in a hurricane. However, the party was rescued by Byrd, and taken in the Fairchild machine in two flights back to the base.

Gould found the Rockefeller Range to consist of no less than forty peaks extending in crescent-shape open to the westward from 77° 35′ S., 153° 5′ W. to 78° 14′ S., 155° 15′ W.

During the winter full plans were drawn up and broadcast. The leading features were Byrd's flight to the South Pole; a geological journey to Queen Maud Mountains (which Amundsen had discovered); and further investigations to the eastward of King Edward VII Land.

Press accounts of this wonderful expedition referred to it as the Million Dollar Antarctic Expedition. It certainly was costly ; how could it have been otherwise ? To-day Australia is, as already stated, embarking on a one and a half million pound Antarctic enterprise. It will be interesting to hear what Byrd's 1946–47 " Operation High Jump " Antarctic Expedition has cost the United States Treasury. Whatever may be said on the subject, the Western Powers to-day should agree that this intricate investigation of Antarctica is well worth while. It must be undertaken, lest the international situation should deteriorate, *which God forbid*, and result in a " cold war ".

Yes, it had to be undertaken and I shall have something to say about it later on. But to continue with Byrd's " Little America " story—before the actual South Polar flight in the big Ford monoplane, which was named the *Floyd Bennett*, test-hops were made and a base-laying flight carried out from which Byrd saw the Barrier, smooth, undulating and relentless, like a vast frozen desert stretching for ever southward.

The *Floyd Bennett*, flying at an altitude of 1,200 feet, passed over depots that had been laid out and over a terribly crevassed area between 81° and 82° S. latitude, and suddenly McKinley sighted, and pointed out to his leader, five sledge teams which he knew were Gould's geological party.

" Must be cold down there " he yelled whilst the plane dipped in salute, and passed them at 300 feet.

Byrd so aptly says in his book : " If ever a conclusive contrast was struck between the new and the old methods of Polar travelling, it was then."

A bag of letters and oddments was dropped, and on went the *Floyd Bennett* at a speed per hour which equalled eight days' foot-slogging.

New peaks rising above the horizon, new glaciers carving their way between high mountains and down to the white Ice Barrier. One of these glaciers, larger and more beautiful than the rest, was the Beardmore, up which Shackleton's men and twelve of our people in Scott's southern journey had dragged sledges laden with supplies. Then came the Queen Maud Range ". . . a solid mass of mountains cut and riven by glacial streams. Here, indeed, was what we had come so far to see ".

Spread out on the navigational table, says Byrd, were Amundsen's charts, a number of photographs torn from his book, and scribbled notes taken from his descriptions.

Here Byrd says that he recognized nothing. The *Floyd Bennett* was heading for what he took to be Axel Heiberg Glacier.

Soon after he sighted Mount Nansen, up till then considered to be 15,000 feet in altitude, and then even higher mountain masses were sighted and a little while later Dean Smith, the pilot, brought the big plane down as coolly as if he were landing on some large level aerodrome. (In the 1946–47 Naval Air Expedition to Antarctica, the most modern methods and instruments have generally given even higher altitudes to most of the big peaks already discovered.)

On November 18, 1929, a fuelling depot was established at the foot of the mountains over which the *Floyd Bennett* must fly to the Pole itself. Then, taking off once more and failing to find Amundsen's Carmen Land, Byrd flew some way to the eastward, and incidentally extended the known limits of the Great Ice Barrier for 100 miles in that direction. Further search and examination of the new mountain ranges they had sighted were brought to a halt by the discovery that the fuel supply was " dangerously low ". A leak had developed in the petrol tank near the fuel pump underneath the pilot's seat, and Byrd was compelled to turn northward and make for Little America.

Flying at about 2,000 feet at economical speed they came back, and, only just clearing the worst crevassed area, Dean Smith made a safe landing about 100 miles south of Little America.

It was an exciting time, a very exciting time indeed, but, thanks to W/T communication, Balchen, with Petersen, his radio-operator, flew out in the Fairchild machine, landed and transferred 100 gallons of petrol to the *Floyd Bennett*. After some further excitements the big Ford monoplane, helped by a southerly wind, reached Little America, and soon afterwards started on the Polar flight.

Thanksgiving Day, November 25, 1929, found Bernt Balchen at the controls, and, as Byrd says : " in his element." With this renowned Polar pilot, McKinley as surveyor, Harold June as W/T operator and relief pilot, and Byrd as navigator and commander, the South Polar flight was begun, at 3.29 a.m. Flying southward on the meridian of 143° 45' W. the three-engined Ford monoplane passed over the earlier depots on the Barrier, until it came to the northern edge of the bad crevasses, then followed the meridian of 164° W. and continued making southing until the Queen Maud Range was sighted ahead.

Soon after 8 a.m. Gould's geological party was seen looking like "a cluster of little beetles", and then dropping to an altitude of about 750 feet photographs of the Queen Maud Range were parachuted down, according to promise, and the Ford rose again, flying steadily southward on the 164th meridian—climbing, climbing, climbing, until at 9 a.m. an altitude of 9,000 feet had been reached.

Still rising and with just enough petrol to take Byrd and his party to the Pole and back, and the altimeter showing 9,600 feet—still slowly climbing "but at a rapidly diminishing rate of speed . . . the heavy plane responded to the controls with marked sluggishness ".

Byrd's account states that it was an awesome thing creeping, so it seemed, through the narrow pass with the black walls of Mts. Nansen and Fisher on either side, needing more power, for the *Floyd Bennett* in its present loaded condition and trim was at its ceiling.

How thrilling, how exciting and hazardous that South Polar flight must have been.

There is a photograph " Over the Hump " taken by Captain McKinley showing the plane over the head of the pass of Liv's Glacier on the way to the Pole, altitude over 10,000 feet.

The situation had become critical ; the plane was unable to climb quickly enough to clear the summit of the pass without lightening her. Balchen held on to the last degree of safety, then began to shout and gesticulate —200 lb. weight must go at once—either food or petrol ; if petrol they could never get back to their base. If food it meant risking their lives in the event of a forced landing. Byrd was responsible. He must decide and he did. Out went a 125 lb. food bag through the trap-door. An immediate improvement in the flying was noticeable, and the climb was renewed, but it was obvious that further lightening was necessary and quickly. "Another bag " shouted Bernt Balchen.

Down went another 250 lb. of food—a month's sledging that meant.

Down went the food and up went the plane.

Flying at seventy-seven nautical miles per hour through the pass, they " cleared the dreaded ' Hump ' at last ", as Byrd remarks in his thrilling account.

Now, at 9.45 a.m. the Pole lay 300 miles ahead of them, and turning due south with a huge chain of 15,000 feet mountains skirting the edge of the bleak inland plateau, Byrd made straight for the Pole, flying south on the 171st meridian W.

Making slight navigational adjustments to allow for a variable wind from the east, and flying over that bleak plateau at ninety miles an hour at approximately 1,100 feet altitude, Byrd says : " It was difficult to believe that in recent history the most resolute men who had ever attempted to carry a remote objective, Scott and Shackleton, had plodded over this same plateau, a few miles each day with hunger—fierce, unrelenting hunger —stalking them every step of the way."

By 1.14 p.m. (Greenwich time) calculations showed that the party was over the South Pole.

One of Captain McKinley's photographs taken 2,000 feet above the Polar plateau, and say 11,000 feet above sea level, shows the sastrugi, or wind-waves, thereabouts, and reminds me of my 1,500 mile long sledge journey across Barrier and glacier and plateau, nearly forty years ago.

Unfortunately for me, on the only occasion when I had the honour of meeting Byrd it was during the second Great World War, when I had just been called away from a party at the Savoy by an urgent message requiring me to rush to an " incident ". There were so many questions I wanted to ask and I wished to thank this great American explorer-admiral for dropping the British and the Norwegian flags over the desolate South Pole, in tribute to my own grand leader, and to the valiant Norseman who had reached the uttermost south only a few weeks before Scott.

The nature of this volume does not give space enough to describe Dr. Gould's very fine geological journey to the Queen Maud Mountains, but the chapter would be incomplete if I failed to set down Admiral Byrd's modest summing up of this great adventure. He says: "One gets there, and that is about all there is for the telling. It's the effort to get there that counts."

Chapter Fourteen

THE GRAHAM LAND EXPEDITION

THE British Graham Land Expedition, 1934–37, was a young man's expedition, a modern young man's expedition, led by a young Australian, John Rymill. Most of the work of the expedition was carried out in the Graham Land sector, which is about the meridian of 65° W. longitude, within and without the Antarctic Circle.

Contrasted with Byrd's Antarctic expedition it was a remarkably economical undertaking.

Bellingshausen in 1821, Larsen in 1893, De Gerlache 1898, Nordenskjöld 1902, Charcot in 1909, Wilkins 1928–29, the *William Scorsby* in 1929, and *Discovery II* in 1931 had all had a finger in the Graham Land pie ; but Rymill's young men certainly broke the crust and ate their fill.

The description in the leader's book is most readable. Rymill is frank in his criticisms and fair in his appreciation. The *Penola*, named after Rymill's home in beautiful sun-kissed South Australia, was a three-masted fore-topsail schooner, fitted with two 50 h.p. Junker Diesel engines.

The whole expedition only cost £20,000.

The time was very well spent ; everybody was busy at his special subject, yet always with an eye on co-operation, which is the foundation of successful exploration.

The photography and chart work were admirable.

The care and management of the dogs, and the psychological appreciation of their sledge-dog value, their tempers and their staying powers was particularly well

143

studied by Surgeon Lieutenant-Commander E. W. Bingham, whose most interesting account in Rymill's book emphasizes that the forty-five pups born during the time spent at the Argentine islands were the backbone of the dog teams during the long sledge journeys made when they were hardly a year old.

Rymill paid about £3,000 for the *Penola* which was what we paid for the *Morning* National Antarctic Relief Expedition ship thirty-two years before. Both ships were about the same age, 32, when in 1902 and 1934 they sailed out of " Old Father Thames " on their way to the desolate Antarctic—*but* what one could buy for £3,000 in 1902 was a great deal more valuable from the seaman-explorer's viewpoint than that which could be purchased in 1934 !

Rymill appointed Lieutenant Ryder, R.N. (the first Antarctic explorer to win the V.C.) to command the *Penola*. At the time of writing Ryder, now Captain Ryder, V.C., R.N., is naval attaché in Norway, and since the British Graham Land expedition owes so much to the Norwegians this seems to be a well-considered appointment.

The British Graham Land expedition's first year, from February, 1935, to February, 1936, was spent in the Argentine islands, the " Northern Base " being in the S.E. corner of Winter Island in latitude 65° 15′ S., longitude 64° 16′ W., the shore party building the winter hut, and *Penola* moving into her winter quarters nearby.

Before the end of February, 1935, the seaplane, a Dragon-Moth, made a flight southward at an altitude of 3,000 feet. Rymill describes a " magnificent view of awe-inspiring scenery " but says " our hopes of finding any sledging routes soon faded away, for even the promontories were fringed with narrow glaciers ending in ice-cliffs. Farther into the bays, these narrow glaciers gave place to broad crevassed ones, or to rocky cliffs where the mountains came to the water's edge. The backs of the bays terminated in steep valley glaciers, which flowed down from a large glacier running parallel to and at the foot of the great plateau scarp. This large glacier was fed by tremendous ice-falls which, in places, poured over the 4,000-foot sheer rock-wall of the central Graham Land plateau. One or two of these ice-falls looked as if they could be climbed, but only by a small party travelling as light as possible ".

On Rymill's homeward flight, he looked down on the sea, and upon the great icebergs which from the Dragon-Moth appeared like tiny sheets of white paper floating in the blue water. He learnt a lot from this flight and saw that it would be difficult, well-nigh impossible, to get sufficient supplies on to the high central plateau to make long journeys to the south or east possible, and that their exploration work must necessarily be confined to the Bellingshausen Sea side of Graham Land.

Short sledge journeys, motor-boat trips and flights were, however, undertaken ; depots were laid out and a great deal added to our knowledge of the Graham Land sector, and preparations were made for the main sledging journeys.

The aircraft was used for exploratory flights to very good purpose.

The mapping undertaken by various parties put a somewhat changed face on the charts of earlier explorers and the straits which divided Graham Land from the mainland were proved not to exist, or, rather, to be valleys filled with glacier-ice.

It is interesting to compare the Norwegian chart showing Larsen's, Nordenskjöld's and Wilkins' discoveries, 1893, 1902, 1928, 1930, together with the *Jason's* and *Hertha's* tracks after Friedrichsen's chart and J. Petersen's description in his article, " The Norwegian Discoveries in Western Antarctica, 1893 ", with the British Graham Land Expedition's chart of Graham Land made between January, 1935, and March, 1937.

From this latter and obviously more detailed chart Crane Channel, Casey Channel, Lurabee Channel and the Finley Islands all go out and Alexander I Island has its name changed to Alexander I Land, which Rymill finds to be some three hundred miles long instead of fifty ; but this is nothing to the original chart of the Dirck Gherritz Archipelago, produced by the Oceana Steamship Co. in Hamburg in 1893. What will young Rymill say when he looks at the map containing the flight tracks of Byrd's exploring planes, and the illuminating perspective chart of Antarctica, as if seen from a point high over the South Pacific Ocean ? In both these Graham Land is not shown at all, under that name, but as the " Palmer Peninsula ! "

Rymill and his companions found various fossil specimens, plants and shells, and as in Scott's expeditions dry valleys with dust and fossils, limestones, sandstones, and shales, filled with plant remains, which they describe as " a veritable geologist's paradise ".

The time signal system put this expedition's longitude observations on a much more accurate and reliable footing than any of the earlier Antarctic expeditions hereabouts.

Southern Lights, the story of the British Graham Land Expedition, is an attractive book, and in fact one of my favourites. Fortunately the wireless set kept its members in touch with such things as " thoughts from abroad on a Sunday evening cold supper ". Stephenson writes one night :

It was a glorious evening, and I knelt down by the set and was soon completely absorbed in listening to a broadcast of a public meeting in Europe . . . for five minutes I was back in Europe. Slowly, however, I became conscious of the things in front of me, and then suddenly I looked up, and the full beauty of my surroundings came upon me as if I had suddenly been transported here. To the east the silvery mountains cut clearly into a dark-blue sky, whilst to

146

the west the ice-covered mountains and glaciers were flood-lit by the long rays of the setting sun. Everywhere was complete calm and silence ; there was not a sound from the other tent, and only occasionally did a dog stir, make himself a bit more comfortable, and then bury his head again amidst his paws and tail. We were further south than anybody else in the world, and apart from our companions at the base, there was no human being within 1,500 miles. It made one feel extremely insignificant to see and think of such vast areas untouched by man, and in which man had had no influence whatsoever. However, I took the liberty of calling in the help of the transmitter from Washington, and with this time-signal and the sun observation I had made during the day, I was able to add the position of this lonely yet wonderful spot to man's plan of the Earth.

That human touch brought the value of wireless very much home to me. Fortunately, we have excellent reception where I am writing this pot-pourri of Antarctic desolation and adventure—how Mawson and Byrd and others who have lived through the later Antarctic expeditions must have enjoyed listening-in to civilization before the second Great World War, before the tormenting chaos of a world which has, I fear, changed so much for the worse.

Rymill and his expedition mates, like myself, had a very good opinion of Charcot, and it was by a fateful coincidence that, when looking over Marguerite Bay, they received the sad news of the death of Dr. J. B. Charcot, the pioneer explorer thereabouts—Scott's " gentleman of the Pole ".

The *Penola* left for the southern base on February 17, 1936, and, after visiting the newly charted Debenham Islands, went on to the Falklands, arriving at Port Stanley on March 21.

The southern base was established in Marguerite Bay, in the Debenham Islands, and from here various flights and sledge journeys were made to carry out the

general programme that Rymill drew up in consultation
with his second-in-command, Hampton, and Lieutenant
Ryder, and Stephenson, his chief surveyor. They seem
to have been a really good lot of chaps and I find it
refreshing to meet any of them as I now occasionally do
in England, Australia, and in Norway.

The main sledge journey started on September 5,
1936, a bit early from a comfort viewpoint. Stephenson
and Hampton made a reconnaissance flight above
what is King George VI Sound the day before, and from
this now noted that the Sound seemed to be from five to ten
miles in width, and that there was a solid wall of mountains to the west, running up to about 8,000 feet in
height, but they could not see what lay beyond. To the
eastward it was more open, gently rising to 5,000 feet
when well inland : glaciers, valleys, bad crevasses and
bare rocky mountain ranges.

Owing to the distance from the base this pioneer
reconnaissance flight only permitted the aviators to go
forty miles up King George VI Sound, but the view from
the air gave those who were to follow by sledge a good
idea of the nature of the land to the southward and
westward, and of the size of the ice-filled Sound.

Stephenson was able to indicate where large cracks
in the sea-ice and big pools of open water made sledging
impossible. The two fliers reached latitude 70° 10′ S.
and could certainly see as far as 70° 30′ but there was no
indication of any strait, or channel, coming through
from the Weddell Sea, to the eastward, Casey Channel,
charted as being in latitude 69½°, certainly was not there.

Stephenson and Hampton returned as nearly as possible by the same route but " searched the country in
behind the headland (? Cape Jeremy) at the entrance to
the Sound, to see whether we could possibly sledge that
way and so avoid the open water. . . . The mountains
were ice-covered, rose to about 2,500 feet and looked
passable. . . . Providing we could get on to the shelf-

ice it seemed quite an easy route over the col and down into the Sound ". They made a rough sketch-chart showing what they considered to be the best route to follow to avoid the crevasses caused by the glaciers which they had seen on the land side and the rifts caused by movement of the shelf-ice (which was named after Wordie of the *Discovery* Committee and a veteran Polar explorer) on the side nearest the sea. Fortunately, thanks to this reconnaissance flight, they saw, about ten miles south of the conspicuous Cape Berteaux, a large bay where the shelf fell in a gradual slope to sea-level, and really picked on the only easy way up from the frozen sea, which was of vast help to the sledgers.

Rymill, generous leader as he proved himself to be, gave the command of the southern sledge party to Stephenson from a position close to Cape Jeremy.

Rymill left next day, September 5, 1936, from the southern base with two sledge parties, having with him Stephenson, Fleming and Bertram, complete with a dog-team, as one party, whilst Bingham and he each with his own dog-team made up the other.

Stephenson on the southern journey came down on to the ice-filled King George VI Sound on October 16, reached latitude 71° 30', and found no signs of " the mythical Stefansson Strait " which, like the Casey Channel and the Lurabee Channel, is so plainly delineated on the Norwegian chart of the West Antarctic Island Group, and which shows the Norwegian discoveries hereabouts.

Continuing through the narrowest part of the Sound, they found that it curved round to the south-west and widened very considerably. On the 19th the party reached latitude 72°, when, in a position from which they could see that Alexander I Island had extended southward for about 300 miles, Stephenson writes :

Our position of 72° S. and 67° 18' W. put us 70 miles inland on the existing map. It was thought that the edge of the Continent, in about 71°, ran approximately in an east and west direction, but it was quite obvious to us that at any rate as far south as 72° 30' the main trend of the coast was still in a north-south direction, and that beyond that latitude, although we could not see it, the coast probably turned gradually into a south-west direction.

The southern sledge journey, combined with what Stephenson had seen whilst flying, proved that between latitude 67° and 72°—i.e. the whole length of Graham Land—there is no break through from the Bellings-hausen Sea to the Weddell Sea.

On October 19, Stephenson and his party had been away from the base for forty-five days, and had covered nearly 300 miles—a very fine effort. They returned to the base on November 19, after seventy-five days' absence, during which time they had covered 600 miles, and mapped 500 miles of coastline, 450 miles of which had never before been sighted.

Rymill and Bingham, when they parted from Stephenson on September 24, 1936, sledged back to the base—a distance of 90 miles. There had been a change in the original plan resulting in the leader (Rymill) handing over their own provisions, thus enabling Stephenson's party to proceed on September 24 with eight weeks' full supplies for themselves and their dogs to get back to Terra Firma Island, where a depot was arranged for so that Stephenson's party could, if necessary, replenish and themselves get back to the base.

Rymill and Bingham started on the east-south east journey with two dog-teams on October 26, 1936, and were away until January 5, 1937. Following the track taken by the southern party to a point approximately 69° 35' S. and longitude 68° W. and having the good fortune to meet Stephenson's party on November 11 and hear how much had been accomplished, Rymill decided to try and make the first crossing of Graham Land and if possible explore some of its east coast.

This final sledge journey brought Rymill right up on to the as-yet-unvisited Graham Land plateau, which starts to the south of the Wordie shelf-ice, rising gradually to a height of 7,500 feet. Rymill and Bingham met with a good deal of bad weather, and were compelled to do a lot of relaying, which is heartbreaking work.

On November 24 they were well into the mountains and pitched their highest camp at 7,500 feet, abreast of a 9,500 foot mountain, which has been named Mount Wakefield. This was the highest peak that the expedition discovered in Graham Land, and is a very fine-looking mountain indeed.

On November 28 rock specimens were collected and astronomical observations taken and a wireless time signal obtained. They had some trouble in crevassed areas and had the misfortune to lose Bingham's leading dog, who broke through a snow-bridge, and, biting out of his harness, disappeared into the darkness below. Another of Bingham's dogs fell down a crevasse, and also came out of his harness, but landed on a ledge 30 feet down. Rymill rescued him quickly by dropping a running noose on the end of an alpine rope over his head and the heavy animal, pulled up by the neck for thirty feet, was none the worse for it.

On December 8 hard winds, falling snow and drifts made travelling impossible. The snow piled up in soft drifts and ridges, and they were held up for three days. On the fourth day, although travelling was possible, the wind blew hard and reached gale force. Rymill pays a great tribute to his stout-hearted companion, Surgeon Lieutenant-Commander E. W. Bingham, who, despite a painful knee injury, supported him on this remarkable and dangerous sledge journey, which covered a distance of 535 miles and resulted in adding a wealth of information about the desolate Antarctic.

The members of the British Graham Land Expedition took great risks, sledging over broken sea-ice, dog-sledging over cruelly-crevassed plateaux, flying to very good purpose in their Dragon-Moth machine—one must admire the way it was handled and the way the fliers put all their trust in that tiny two-bladed propeller that looks more like a couple of paper-knife blades than a means of carrying out flights of two hundred miles over valleys of cloud and ice, to say nothing of the added danger of a forced landing in the mountains.

My friend, the late Lord Leverhulme, one of the Expedition's supporters, had occasion to fly with me from Hendon to Hawarden Aerodrome, near Birkenhead, in 1943—we were met by his wife at Hawarden, and she appeared quite shocked that I should risk her husband's valuable life in a fragile little " Moth ". Lord Leverhulme pointed out that my life was valuable to my family, as well, and I couldn't help chuckling when I thought of those splendid young explorers who had carried stores on depot-laying trips in a similar small machine, explored in hard wind and bitter-cold weather again and again, and truly used the machine and braved the dangers of the Antarctic in it with no more concern than a schoolgirl using a bicycle.

Whilst on the subject of Graham Land and various explorers' and whaling captains' discoveries in this locality, which several nations have been concerned in, I must not omit Otto Nordenskjöld and Captain C. A. Larsen (the former in the whaler *Antarctic* and the latter in the *Jason*) who did so much on the eastern side of the Graham Land Peninsula and in the Weddell Sea,

Captain Larsen, on December 6, 1893, in the whaler *Jason* penetrated well beyond latitude 68° and plotted the lie of the coast and also mapped the Christensen and Larsen Ice Barriers.

Otto Nordenskjöld in the *Antarctic*, conveying the Swedish Expedition of 1901–04, was landed with three scientists and two sailors on Snow Hill Island, where he wintered in 1902. The party built a timber hut in latitude 64° 25′ S. and the expeditionary ship under Captain C. A. Larsen's command then went north to carry out biological and other research work in the open sea. She was due to return after the winter, but unfortunately she was caught in the ice in Erebus and Terror Gulf, and so badly damaged that she had to be abandoned. The Swedish flag was left flying in her, and soon afterwards she sank.

Nordenskjöld from his winter-quarters carried out several important sledge journeys, including one to explore the land to the westward round the base of Mount Haddington on Ross Island. On this journey he suddenly " encountered two beings from whom the dogs fled howling, and the leader with difficulty recognized them as human. They were black from head to foot, with long black hair hanging down over their shoulders and black bushy beards. They were Dr. Gunnar Andersson and Lieutenant Duse, who had left the *Antarctic* during the previous summer, when it was clear that she could not reach the winter camp, and endeavoured to make their way to it on foot. They had been obliged to build a hut to winter in and to eke out their scanty provisions with seal blubber which was also their only fuel. The united party returned to Snow Hill and resumed the diligent geological and natural history survey of the locality, while waiting anxiously for the ship ".

On November 8, 1903, Captain Irizar and one of the officers of the Argentine gun-boat *Uruguay* were seen approaching the winter-quarters on Snow Hill Island and the same night Captain Larsen also arrived with five of his shipwrecked men.

As Hugh Robert Mill states in his *Siege of the South Pole* :

At last on November 10, 1903, all were reunited on the *Uruguay*, and a week later Captain Irizar had the pride and satisfaction of completing in Tierra del Fuego one of the shortest and most brilliantly successful relief expeditions in Polar History.

Chapter Fifteen

AURORA

THE uttermost South, 90° S., the South Pole, is a fixed point, it stays where it is ; whereas its fickle cousin, the South Magnetic Pole, like the Aurora moves its position continually.

Ross put the Magnetic Pole roughly in latitude 75° S., 154° E., while he also put Gauss's theoretical position about 150 geographical miles to the NNW. He marked on his chart the position assigned by Duperry some 270 miles to the WSW.

Mawson, in Shackleton's *Nimrod* Expedition, by absolute observation fixes the Magnetic Pole in 72° 25′ S., longitude 155° 16′ E. In Mawson's *Aurora* Expedition the position of the Magnetic Pole was approximately in 70° 36′ S., 148° 10′ E., while Bernacchi in the Southern Cross Expedition gives 73° S. 146° E.

And the various Antarctic physicists and magnetic observers, with their dip circles and unifilar magnetometers and delicate instruments of precision, have had some bitterly cold experiences.

Drygalski's physicists in the *Gauss* Expedition in 1902 built an observatory out of ice-blocks. Simpson and Wright in Scott's last expedition had magnetic instruments in an ice-cave.

The Aurora Australis, or Southern Lights, gave us something beautiful and awe-inspiring to look at and talk about, and Wilson managed to produce some realistic and dainty water-colour sketches of the aurora as well as of other natural phenomena, such as mock-suns, earth-shadows, opalescent clouds, and mirage at sunset.

My own best memory of the Aurora Australis, this

most beautiful thing in Antarctica, was in a spring sledging journey in September, 1911, after shivering in my sleeping bag in a temperature as low as minus 73·3 degrees Fahr. out on the Great Ice Barrier.

My little party thought we had had enough of it, and as our work was completed, after making some hot tea, we struck camp and started on a night journey of thirty-five miles to the shelter afforded by the old magnetic hut left by Scott's first expedition near Cape Armitage.

I described the scene in *South With Scott*, for as we moved off, steering by the stars :

We witnessed a magnificent auroral display and as we dragged the now light sledge onward we watched the gold white streamers waving and playing in the heavens. The atmosphere was extraordinarily clear, and we seemed to be marching in fairyland, but for the cold which made our breath come in gasps. We were cased lightly in ice about the shoulders, loins and feet, and we were also covered with the unpleasant rime which our backs had brushed off from the tent walls when we had camped. On we went, however, confident but silent. No other sound now but the swish, swish of our ski as we sped through the soft new snow. In the light of the aurora objects stood out with the razor-edge sharpness of an after-blizzard atmosphere, and the temperature seemed to fall even lower than at midnight. Our fingers seemed to be cut with the frost-burn and frost-bites played all round our faces, making us wince with pain.

We were marching, as it were, under the shadow of Erebus, the great Antarctic volcano, and on this never-to-be-forgotten night the Southern Lights played for hours. If for nothing else, it was worth making such a sledge journey to witness the display. First, vertical shafts ascended in a fan of electric flame, and then the shafts all merged into a filmy, pale chrome sheet. This faded and intensified alternately, and then in an instant disappeared, but more flaming lights burst into view in other parts of the heavens, and a phantom curtain of glittering electric violet trembled between the lights and the stars.

No wonder Wilson and Bowers stated that the Aurora effects were much better and more variegated in colour this southern side of Mount Erebus. The awful splendour of this majestic vision gave us all a most eerie feeling and we forgot our fatigue and the cold whilst we watched.

The Southern Lights continued for some hours, only vanishing with the faint appearance of dawn.

Captain Scott says in his " Auroral Notes " :

The auroral light is of a palish green colour, but we now see distinctly a red flush preceding the motion of any bright part.

The green ghostly light seems suddenly to spring to life with rosy blushes. There is infinite suggestion in this phenomenon, and in that lies its charm ; the suggestion of life, form, colour and movement never less than evanescent, mysterious—no reality. It is the language of mystic signs and portents—the inspiration of the gods—wholly spiritual —divine signalling. Remindful of superstition, provocative of imagination. Might not the inhabitants of some other world (Mars) controlling mighty forces thus surround our globe with fiery symbols, a golden writing which we have not the key to decipher ?

Scott expressed some disappointment that Ponting, our truly expert camera-artist, confessed his inability to obtain photographs of the Aurora Australis, observing that the Norwegian Professor Størmer had been suc cessful in getting some.

Chapter Sixteen

" OPERATION HIGH JUMP "

To Rear-Admiral Richard E. Byrd of the United States Navy should go the highest class of the Order of the Aurora Australis, if that decoration existed! Byrd has led five Polar expeditions, five modern Polar expeditions, of which three have been made in the desolate Antarctic. He is the Air Chief Marshal of Antarctica, and, what's more, he calls the desolate Antarctic an " Enchanted Continent " !

The mere fact that he has flown over both Poles doesn't appear to Admiral Byrd more noteworthy than winning a couple of fleet obstacle-races would to a midshipman.

Naval training and research have now reached such a pitch that in the immediate post-war years an all-naval expedition carried out this " Operation High Jump ", which must have been a gigantic eye-opener to the educated, thinking world.

To Polar explorers living to-day, it must have been the greatest of all surprises.

To the spirit of the Vikings, all down the ranks of Antarctic venturers and explorers who have bowed and gone their way, " Operation High Jump " must be reckoned as the " Miracle of Valhalla ".

In 1946–47 thirteen ships, manned by 4,000 men, carried out this vast project, which included the encircle-ment of the Antarctic Continent, exploration of the coast and the launching of planes from seaplane tenders to make flights inland.

Another major objective was to establish a base like Little America for land-planes fitted with ski for making

157

long reconnaissance, mapping and photographic flights over the unmapped interior of the Antarctic Continent.

Little America was in fact used once more, and from this snowed-under, abandoned Barrier town twenty-nine photographic flights were made. Thirty-five seaplane flights, for similar purposes, were made.

When, on Christmas afternoon, 1902, in my watch on deck, the little relief ship *Morning* sighted Scott Island in latitude 67° 24′ S., longitude 179° 55′ W. and I spent some hours fixing its position astronomically, sounding round it and making water-colour sketches from the crow's nest, while Captain Colbeck landed, hoisted the Union Jack and took possession in the name of King Edward VII, I little thought that forty-four years later a seaplane tender would make this lonely Island the jumping-off place for the Western Group of three naval ships doing a great Naval and Air Exercise, and also that its Central Group of five more ships under a U.S. Admiral would make Scott Island its rendezvous.

Anyway, to-day I can sit in a comfortable chair, with an open perspective map of Antarctica before me, with Scott Island in the centre, and the whole of the desolate Antarctic spread out showing in magnificent simplicity what this mighty United States air, ice and world explorer Admiral Richard Byrd has achieved.

Names conspicuous upon this cleverly designed picture-map conjure up many of those whom I have known and worked with and for. And, having served loyally under five sovereigns since I became a naval officer, it interests me to see :

Victoria Land
Edward VII Land (or Peninsula)
George V Land
Queen Mary Land
Edward VIII Bay
Queen Alexandra Land
Queen Maud Land

Prince Olav Coast
Princess Martha Coast
Princess Astrid Coast
Princess Ragnhild Coast
Prince Harald Coast

and King George VI Sound, by His Majesty's permission, will now adorn the post-war chart of the Antarctic.

Byrd has been modest enough, but Marie Byrd Land, Ellsworth Highland, American Highland, and Wilkes Land, Amundsen Sea, Ross Sea, Bellingshausen Sea and Weddell Sea, Scott Land, Scott Glacier, Scott Island, Commonwealth Range and Bay, and let us hope some outstanding features truly worthy of Mawson, Shackleton and of Admiral Byrd himself will bring this picture-map up to date.

Byrd calls Antarctica a " Sermon in Ice ". Those who have followed his magic career will find it difficult to pay him adequate tribute. In " Operation High Jump " he employed not only the Armed Aircraft-carrying Ice-breaker, but even the submarine, the tractor, the life-saving immersion suit, the freighter, the largest planes ever launched from the carrier, and many marvellous instruments, such as the airborne magnetometer, which could actually determine the nature of the rock under the great 1,500 foot thick ice-cap, and many of the powerful new weapons and instruments which are the heritage of the second Great World War.

Nothing seems to have been forgotten. All the scientific branches applicable were studied and provided for, geographical, hydrographical, meteorological, geological, glacial and even biological, for Byrd thinks on a grand scale, and yet makes provision for the collection of such minute things as phyto-plankton.

To see the film *The Secret Land* is one of my immediate ambitions when I return to London. Byrd's pictures and coloured photographs which I have with me show tractors dragging ten or a dozen sledges across the ice, carrying the working parties and even construction-battalion men, dozens of them, to work on the camp sites. The tractors are very much like those we have up here in the Norwegian mountains, which in principle are the same as Scott's motor tractors or sledges, with which in 1911 he dragged stores from ship to base and from base over the frozen sea and miles out on to the Great Ice Barrier—much improved by experience, and our far greater knowledge of air-cooled engines and metallurgy.

Admiral Byrd's latest exploration is to us " old " Antarctics " the best imaginable translation of the word " miracle ". 4,000,000,000,000,000,000,000,000,000 tons of ice, he says, cover the desolate Antarctic. His figures are astronomical yet he knows what he is talking about.

Whilst writing a personal message to Fleet Admiral Nimitz in Washington when he was quietly " circling the South Pole ", Byrd remarks that the temperature is 40° below zero, their altitude 12,000 feet (2,000 feet above the Pole) and that they are dropping on the Pole the flags of the United Nations. He adds " the young men with me join in sending to you and to the Secretary of the Navy our gratitude for giving us this opportunity for geographical discovery and great adventure. . . ."

POSTSCRIPT

NEW YEAR'S DAY, 1950, marks fifty years of modern Antarctic exploration, fifty years of real progress, fifty years of international co-operation, which include the siege and conquest of the South Pole, the introduction of motor transport, aircraft and aircraft carriers, and even submarines, and last, but by no means least, wireless, radar and the many discoveries developed during two great world wars, which can be made use of for scientific investigation in that six million square mile area bounded by the Antarctic Circle.

In Scott's day, when the stoutly-built *Discovery* anchored in Arrival Bay, McMurdo Sound, her crew saw the sea freezing over as the days grew shorter and darker, and night shadows of cruel dark purple added to the natural gloom of that very lonely land.

There was no wireless fitted to the low-powered auxiliary craft that were then used for Antarctic exploration, and when the sun disappeared below the northern horizon those who wintered in the South Polar Regions were cut off from the world and alone.

Not so with the *Norsel* men, who will normally be able to send and receive wireless messages, listen to the news at the same time as those in ocean liners and keep in " headlines " touch with civilization. They will be able to get time signals and meteorological reports and a wealth of information that was denied to Scott and his contemporary explorers early in the twentieth century.

As stated briefly, Sir Douglas Mawson, and the Australasian expeditions with which Mawson has been associated, have made use of wireless, and, as far back as 1930, when I commanded the Royal Australian

Squadron, I was able to communicate with Mawson when he was exploring in the vicinity of Enderby Land.

The Australian Government has consulted Mawson through its Antarctic Planning Committee, and at a Cabinet Meeting on August 16, 1947, it was agreed that scientific and meteorological stations should be set up on Heard and Macquarie Islands and maintained for a period of at least five years. It was also agreed that a systematic reconnaissance of the coast of the Australian Antarctic territory should be carried out over a number of years by the *Wyatt Earp* with a view to establishing a permanent scientific station on the Antarctic Continent itself ; and that another ship should be obtained of much greater capacity, especially adapted for work in Antarctic waters.

The *Wyatt Earp's* small size and very low power make her unsuitable for any long-range reconnaissance, and it does seem to me that now is the time to acquire the 12-knot specially constructed *Norsel* for the completion and extension of the exploration of the Antarctic Continent between Adélie Land and Crown Princess Martha Land, or roughly between the meridian of Greenwich and longitude 150° E.

Two important expeditions are now exploring the South Pole—the French Antarctic Expedition on board the *Commandant Charcot*, which has made a landing in Adélie Land, near Cape Discovery, and the Norwegian-British-Swedish Expedition which left London at the beginning of December, 1949, aboard the *Norsel*, a steel sealer, bound for Queen Maud Land, where a party of fourteen men will winter and explore the interior of Antarctica for two years. These fourteen include two British, one Australian and one Canadian. An R.A.F. unit is attached to the expedition, and it is reported to be doing invaluable work reconnoitring passages through the ice, thus saving time and fuel. The international character of the expedition is new, and a most excellent idea, and the nations have contributed towards the cost, although the bulk is borne by Norway. Much fine equipment has been supplied by Britain, including precision instruments, sledges with plastic running surfaces, wind-proof cloth and woollen clothes, cookers, generators and radio gear.

One of the main purposes of this expedition is the scientific investigation of climate. There is evidence that the world's climate is getting warmer, and this is supported by facts such as the expansion of the Northern forests, the better prospects for agriculture in Northern Sweden and Finland, and migration of fish due to the rise in temperature of the Northern currents. In the South, too, there seem to be remarkable changes in conditions. The Germans brought back photographic evidence of snow-free, ice-free regions from their Antarctic flights of 1938–39 over Queen Maud Land, and Commander Hawkes and Captain Bond, in February, 1947, took air photographs showing oases which appear to have a fairly temperate climate during the Antarctic summer. Tucked away in the new mountain ranges which Byrd's airmen discovered are areas quite clear of snow and ice with low black rock hills absorbing a great deal of heat in the summer. Byrd's men described these areas as " regions of new wonders of the world ". And they found a series of isolated mountains whose sides were stratified with rocks of various colours which had something of the appearance of the Great Canyon of Colorado. Thus geological investigation is also planned. Coal, lead, tin, copper, gold and silver have all been found in Antarctica, but further knowledge is needed. Uranium has not yet been traced.

These are but two of the main items for investigation, but there is much to be learned and vast areas of land to explore ; there is excitement and endurance, there is infinite boredom, yet warm good-fellowship for those fourteen men. I long to join them for it would not be

right to say of me, in the words of Robert Louis
Stevenson :

> Billow and breeze, islands and seas,
> Mountains of rain and sun,
> All that was good, all that was fair,
> All that was me is gone.

But I will not be returning. I leave such a life to
others. Perhaps, on that cruel, silent continent they will
feel the spirit of men who have died struggling against
adversity, for no land has witnessed greater fortitude
and bravery in the interests of scientific investigation
and hazardous adventure. And they, too, may agree
with our greatest explorer, " How much better all this
has been than lounging in too great comfort at home ".

BIBLIOGRAPHY

Bjarne Aagaard, *Fangst og Forskning i Sydishavet* (3 vols.), Gyldendal.

Roald Amundsen, *The South Pole* (2 vols.), Murray.

H. G. Armstrong (Ed.), *Tales of Hazard*, Lane.

H. Begbie, *Shackleton—a Memory*, Mills & Boon.

Louis Bernacchi, *To the South Polar Regions*, Hurst & Blackett.

Louis Bernacchi, *Voyage of the Scotia*, Blackwood.

R. E. Byrd, *Little America*, Putnam.

Jean Charcot, *The Voyage of the Why-Not in the Antarctic*, Hodder & Stoughton.

Lars Christensen, *Such is the Antarctic*, Hodder & Stoughton.

J. G. S. Doorly, *In the Wake*, Sampson Low.

Edith L. Elias, *The Book of Polar Exploration*, Harrap.

Lincoln Ellsworth, *Beyond Horizons*, Heinemann.

Karl Fricker, *The Antarctic Regions*, Swan, Sonnenschein.

Stephen Gwynn, *Captain Scott*, Lane.

Helmer Hanssen, *Voyages of a Modern Viking*, Routledge.

J. Gordon Hayes, *The Conquest of the South Pole*, Eyre & Spottiswoode.

F. Hurley, *Argonauts of the South*, Putnam.

E. E. M. Joyce, *The South Polar Trail*, Duckworth.

C. F. Laseron, *South With Mawson*, Harrap.

G. Murray Levick, *Antarctic Penguins*, Heinemann.

Sir Douglas Mawson, *The Home of the Blizzard*, Hodder & Stoughton.

H. R. Mill, *The Siege of the South Pole*, Alston Rivers.

Lord Mountevans, *South With Scott*, Collins.

Lord Mountevans, *British Polar Explorers*, Collins.

Lord Mountevans, *Adventurous Life*, Hutchinson.

Lord Mountevans, *The Mystery of the Polar Star*, Partridge.

Herbert G. Ponting, *The Great White South*, Duckworth.

Sir James Ross, *Voyage to the Southern Seas* (2 vols.), Murray.

Geo. Murray (Ed.), *The Antarctic Manual*, Royal Geographical Society.

R. N. Rudmose Brown, *The Polar Regions*, Methuen.

John Rymill, *Southern Lights*, Chatto & Windus.

Sir Ernest Shackleton, *Shackleton in the Antarctic*, Heinemann.

Sir Ernest Shackleton, *South*, Heinemann.

Captain R. F. Scott, *The Voyage of the Discovery* (2 vols.), Murray.

Captain R. F. Scott, *Scott's Last Expedition*, Murray.

F. Wild, *Shackleton's Last Voyage*, Cassell.

INDEX

166

INDEX

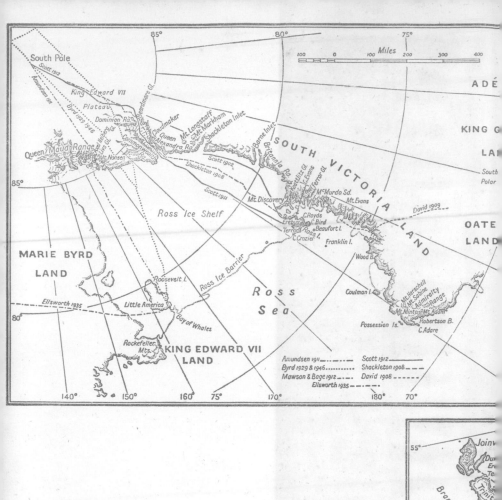

FLYING EXPEDITIONS

INDEX